THE TRAVEL AND TOURISM INDUSTRY

STRATEGIES FOR THE FUTURE

Edited by
ADÈLE HODGSON

PERGAMON PRESS

OXFORD · NEW YORK · BEIJING · FRANKFURT
SAO PAULO · SYDNEY · TOKYO · TORONTO

U.K.	Pergamon Press plc, Headington Hill Hall, Oxford OX3 0BW, England
U.S.A.	Pergamon Press, Inc., Maxwell House, Fairview Park, Elmsford, New York 10523, U.S.A.
PEOPLE'S REPUBLIC OF CHINA	Pergamon Press, Room 4037, Qianmen Hotel, Beijing, People's Republic of China
FEDERAL REPUBLIC OF GERMANY	Pergamon Press GmbH, Hammerweg 6, D-6242 Kronberg, Federal Republic of Germany
BRAZIL	Pergamon Editora Ltda, Rua Eça de Queiros, 346, CEP 04011, Paraiso, São Paulo, Brazil
AUSTRALIA	Pergamon Press Australia Pty Ltd., P.O. Box 544, Potts Point, N.S.W. 2011, Australia
JAPAN	Pergamon Press, 5th Floor, Matsuoka Central Building, 1-7-1 Nishishinjuku, Shinjuku-ku, Tokyo 160, Japan
CANADA	Pergamon Press Canada Ltd., Suite No. 271, 253 College Street, Toronto, Ontario, Canada M5T 1R5

Copyright © 1987 Pergamon Books Ltd

First edition 1987
Reprinted 1988 (with corrections)

Library of Congress Cataloging in Publication Data

The travel and tourism industry.
Includes index.
1. Tourist trade. I. Hodgson, Adèle.
G155.A1T646 1987   380.1'459104   86–25296

British Library Cataloguing in Publication Data

The travel and tourism industry: strategies for the future.
1. Tourist trade
I. Hodgson, Adèle
338.4'791   G155.A1

ISBN 0–08–033892–5 (Hardcover)
ISBN 0–08–033893–3 (Flexicover)

Printed in Great Britain by A. Wheaton & Co. Ltd., Exeter

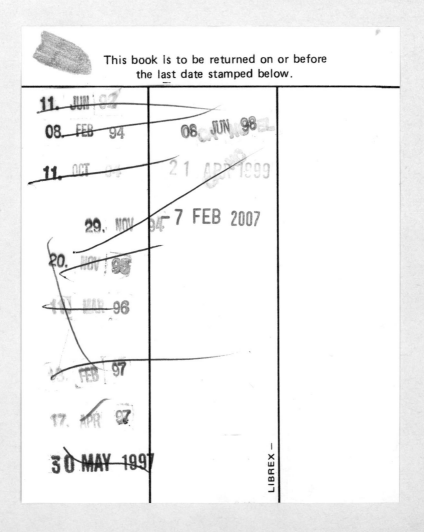

Other Pergamon Titles of Interest

CASEE & REULAND
The Management of Hospitality

DOZ
Strategic Management in Multinational Companies

McNAMEE
Tools and Techniques of Strategic Management

Related Pergamon Journals

Omega

Long Range Planning

Management and Marketing Abstracts

International Journal of Hospitality Management

Contents

Preface

Strategy — Is It Necessary?

More and more organisations are learning to their cost that the only alternative to strategy is the vague, general aim of 'let's make profits'. Sadly, such a philosophy is all too often characterised by a lack of formal objectives and monitoring systems, and by a tendency to seize each opportunity as it comes, regardless of its overall long term impact.

Those who advocate such an approach maintain it allows the company to be more flexible, faster-moving and unrestricted. Strategy, they feel, limits a company's horizons and inhibits the true entrepreneurial spirit. The arguments sound plausible, even sensible, especially when looking at emerging industries. But a close analysis of past experience reveals that, for most companies, the advantages of a planned strategy far outweigh any disadvantages or any other considerations.

In this book we seek to explain exactly why strategy is so essential in today's fiercely competitive environment. Like von Neumann and O I Morgenstern, the first writers on strategy, we hope to show that strategy has two meanings: 'pure strategy' — representing specific moves, for example, product development; and 'mixed strategy' the art of deciding what particular course a company should follow, providing a framework of criteria against which decisions should be made. Simply setting objectives is not enough to foster structured and profitable growth. What is required is a well-defined growth direction based on an analysis of the inherent strengths and weaknesses of the total organisation.

This book is concerned with the travel industry and our objective is to develop a valuable set of practical ideas and observations to help the critical thinking of both student and manager.

The travel industry is very large and complex and our interest lies in seeing it move forward creatively and economically. Thus we have attempted to make our approach pragmatic and practical by drawing on a combination of real life experience and the best of theoretical research.

What we hope has emerged is a book which is just as much at home on the bedside table as it is in the boardroom or classroom.

'Remember, strategy is when you are out of ammunition, but keep right on firing so that the enemy won't know.'

Brusssels 1986

Acknowledgements

This book owes its existence to a meeting in Brussels one sunny September day in 1984. All of us involved owe a great debt not only to our own companies in the travel industry, but also to the many unnamed others who gave help and advice. I am particularly grateful to Global Partners for their input and support.

I wonder if this book would have been started or written without the encouragement we gave to each other? And certainly, our thanks must go to our secretarial helpers, who deciphered, corrected and punctuated our manuscripts.

The views and opinions stated by the contributors do not necessarily reflect the opinions of the organisations they represent: nor can they be held responsible for any errors or omissions.

A.M.H.

1

The Travel Industry —
Its History

IF PEOPLE were asked to nominate a leading sector of the world economy, few would mention the travel industry. There is, amazingly, widespread ignorance of its size and complexity, and of the huge sums of money it generates. The aim of this chapter is, therefore, to give a brief overview of this prosperous industry. In particular, we will examine the type of strategy it has developed, and is likely to develop, to deal with communal and specialised problems.

Like the financial industry, our activities are perhaps too diverse and fragmented to be widely understood. Yet the World Trade Organisation estimates that 3.5 billion people travel the world every year. About 20% of these movements are business trips and, according to a recent survey, business travellers account for up to 50% of the tourist entries into individual countries. By 1988, 16 million visitors to the UK could be spending £7.5 billion.

With such huge sums of money at stake there is keen competition amongst the suppliers and distributors. The market-place has become volatile and the risks tremendous, as greater and greater stress is laid on achieving dominant positions. All fear the innovative newcomer, and market leaders have been known to unite, even to sacrifice profitability, in the fight to limit the interloper's potential.

How then did this massive industry come into being: an industry pioneered by adventurers, heroes and dream-driven inventors, an industry which constantly faces an exciting future and yet is vulnerable to the tragedies of human error, stop-gap strategies and almost hysterical competition?

The evolution has been continuous and often more exciting than fiction — with numerous stories of scandals, takeovers, loss of life and power struggles. Those early entrepreneurs, often with limited financial resources, saw the industry develop till the need arose for colossal outside support — either via Government backing, consortia or stock issue. Even in Europe, a more compact and less dramatic land mass, the sums of capital required to finance land, sea and air transportation grew steadily to astronomical levels.

So, the romantic image of the lonely pioneer surveying isolated, dangerous terrain has been succeeded by the stark reality of stock flotations, loans, budgets and bankruptcies. Over the years, folk heroes have come and gone. Their ideas have, in general, promoted the development of the travel industry but their demise has usually caused financial havoc and prompted stringent, externally imposed controls.

To travel, then, along the paths forged by those pioneers was an adventure — sometimes uncomfortable, but never lacking in glamour or charm. Today, in our efficient technological world, we are herded into almost infantile dependence; lulled by promises, censored information and well-practised smiles. The dreams of the past regarding speed, frequency of service, comfort and global link-ups have become reality. But, today the industry is all too often directed by the bureaucrat. Systems dominate initiative; the gulf between the hierarchical levels has widened and in many instances true innovation has died. Our industry, swamped in a morass of ill-conceived strategies poorly adapted to the needs of the organisation and the consumer, is in danger of losing direction.

Over the years the travel industry has redrawn the contours of our globe; crossing vast countries and continents, opening up the way to traders and industrial development, and strengthening contacts with and control over vast overseas possessions and business empires. Each new technical advance, whether it was the advent of steam, the flying machine, multi-storey hotels or even improved rail track, made possible more comfortable and speedier links with wider markets. The dawning of the revolution in transport gradually engineered the development of markets into those which we describe as 'global'. In the past 80 years, we have seen a worldwide evolution in transport and travel habits which would have been inconceivable to our forebears. This development has been so fast that investment provision has constantly proved inadequate, and failure to plan for the future can prove almost ruinously expensive.

Nowhere in the world is isolated. The realms of space have been conquered and some remote corners of the globe are now accepted holiday centres. Distance is no longer so closely cost-related and the further we travel the greater the bargains. All this has transformed not only world economics but also human lifestyles. Now businessmen fly from one commercial centre to the next, covering thousands of miles in a matter of hours. Some even live in one country and work in another. Flights from Paris to Madrid, for example, are described as 'the milk run'. We can, as individuals, now live at a speed which almost defies description. Our horizons have broadened and the experiences we have gained are making us into more sophisticated and discerning consumers.

No one could have predicted the public demand for cheap mass travel. There were no precedents upon which to base expectations. The phenomenon emerged from the industrialised world's desire to seek new experiences, and the increased availability of disposable income.

In an attempt to understand this phenomenon, let us review how the modern travel industry began — with the railways.

The Railways

The first dramatic change in our styles of travelling came with the railways. The early railways gave people a sense of freedom which facilitated not only social and business activities but also the grim mechanics of war. Armies were able to adopt new strategies by moving not only themselves but also heavy artillery and equipment to far off theatres of destruction. At first, few appear to have appreciated fully the real benefits of this new freedom of movement. Early critics cynically compared rail travel for passengers to the dehumanised process of transporting parcels. I wonder what they would think today?

Train travel, during those early years, became more sophisticated, offering various ancillary services such as hotels, sleeping and restaurant cars. Travel costs were relatively high and yet, throughout the world, the railways became an integral part of everyday life with a definite visual presence. The railway station was part of a line; a route which led to family, friends, business — a social and economic link. The public identified with the train; they could understand railway technology and felt it was part of their heritage. Vital engineering statistics relating to train and track became part of a schoolboy's repertoire, and as those massive monsters, the trains, ploughed across the continents of the world, people rejoiced in their advent and basked in the immediate and long term benefits they brought. With the age of the train the mass movement of people began and Thomas Cook is quoted as saying that his planned tours added much to 'the advancement of human progress'.

In India and the USA, two vast land masses where communications were difficult, train travel offered an opportunity to create countries and communities. It also provided vital routes to the sea ports. Russia, a country where climate, terrain and vastness affected and prevented travel, was another exciting example. The birth of railways helped to hurtle that feudal country into the modern age and the social and economic repercussions reverberated throughout the world. Railways opened up routes through deserts, jungles, mountain ranges and unpopulated plains, and gave communities and countries the chance to develop stronger links with each other. The trains paved the way for the mass tourism which the jet age would bring and the subsequent fierce competition that was to develop for 'bottoms on seats'.

Today, after years of capital starvation, outdated technology and fierce competition, the railways are attempting to do more than just survive. They

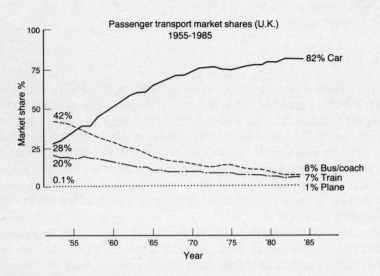

FIG. 1.1. Passenger transport market shares (UK) 1955-85

are fighting to win back an accepted and respected role in our world. The aim is simple — to build up sufficient custom and revenue to become more cost effective and eliminate vast borrowings. A wide variety of methods are being used to promote business and the aims are those of any consumer products manufacturer — 'sell more of the product'! However, freight business, once so lucrative in the USA and parts of Europe, has been lost to the truckers and is unlikely to return.

Most of the present railway investment programme is based on new and faster track, speedier engines and increased customer comfort and care. Jeff Percival, with his unique knowledge of the industry, will present his views on strategy past, present and future, so let it suffice for me to point out that the railways are still besieged by problems and that governments will always have to subsidise uneconomic links to meet social needs. For, despite the new innovations, profits are still terrifyingly elusive. The world is now so full of alternative methods of transport that it has become very hard for the railways to increase market share.

In 1830 the first railway between Liverpool and Manchester was opened and by 1869 the USA was united by the joining of the Union Pacific and the Central Pacific. By 1893, despite the early boom years, approximately half the US railway track and its equipment was in the hands of the receivers. In just over half a century railways had almost lived their active life-span from conception to receivership. US railway companies might have survived in better shape if they had seen themselves as being in the distribution and leisure business rather than simply running railways.

Railways — Reborn?

The laws of free enterprise can not be applied simplistically to the railways. What is required is a consistent strategy developed jointly by management, staff and governments, plus a structured deployment of capital and assets, based on a genuine desire to provide a service. Like most other forms of communication, rail travel, which once seemed so liberating and novel, has become an overcrowded, uncomfortable form of mass transportation. A major obstacle has thus to be overcome when trying to create a new image. So incensed is the weary traveller by dirty, sordid stations in parts of Europe and the USA that he fails to appreciate the actual regularity and efficiency of the service offered, the years of research and planning which have gone into train and track design, and the safe control of traffic.

While railway middle-management develop reclining seats and prepacked airline type meals, which the passengers can eat while using the recently installed phones, the railway senior management are wrestling with pressing problems of another kind, problems related to the policies of government departments. Will governments continue to pay high subsidies? Over the years, the customers have been the casualties of that struggle and they have paid heavily as the victims of that — whether in the form of high fares, lack of regional services or the general contempt of the railways for the traveller.

Railways have always been part of a major political debate, but with imagination and leadership they could again play a vital role in opening up new opportunities and providing more flexible and speedier means of communication. Senior railway management, caught between the dictates of government and the demands of consumers and employees, must come to terms with their future. It is a future to be found, not in the ivory tower of the boardroom, but on the shop floor and out in the field.

Travel will take a tremendous step forward as a social, economic and political influence if all goes according to plan, because in 7 years' time Europeans will be able to travel from East to West without crossing the Channel. The link, a tunnel, will be built by the Channel Tunnel Group and France Manche which will bore two 7.3 metre rail tunnels under the seabed. The consortium, however, in order to proceed with this £2.66 bn. project, had to gain parliamentary approval, raise the money and secure agreements with the British and French rail networks.

Initial demand for this service is expected to be about 1,000 vehicles an hour and should gradually increase. The railway journey will mean that France will be able to run its high-speed TGV trains and, should any strategic decision ever be made on high-speed trains in the UK, then the trip from London to Paris could be more than halved in time. France has made no secret of the fact that it will boost France's high-speed train technology, particularly as TGV links are being forged with Amsterdam, Brussels, Cologne and Stuttgart.

Where is all the money going to come from? Certainly not from the respective governments. About 32 international banks have given commitments for £4.3 bn. in development loans. The return on equity of around £1 bn. is put at 19% and the bank loans will be refinanced through revenue bonds or within 15 years.

The implications for the cross-Channel shipping companies are profound and they promise a fierce battle. It is thought that it will not lead to a fares war but only time will tell. An important aspect of the ferry companies' retaliation strategy will be cutting costs, without damaging service levels, by introducing new larger ferries into service and cutting staff levels.

One final interesting point is that the shuttle would be a private company not belonging to the national railways and, as such, less vulnerable to strikes.

Putting this whole development into context, it is important to see it as another competitive element in the travel industry. Let us hope it will lead to further deregulation on the price and availability of air transport and improvement in the movements of people and products between the countries of Europe.

The Airlines And Their Strategies

The risk-taking, entrepreneurial spirit which characterised the initial development of the railways was also evident in the early days of aviation. Over the years, airlines throughout the world have attracted and even created men of enormous talent — and, sometimes, huge egos. All too often, they were men so mesmerised by their own expertise and business daring that they were too careless about the bottom line: which explains their swift and dramatic falls from profitability and positions of power. This instinct to gamble has, however, more recently been curbed; for increased competition, deregulation, and the major recessions have reined in even the reckless. The heads of airlines now listen to their finance directors and the new rulers of Anthony Sampson's 'Empires of Sky' are themselves more professional, possessing greatly increased business acumen. Running airlines, as our book seeks to illustrate, will always be a risky business: investments are high, technology sophisticated, lead times are long and there are aggressive rivals determined to dominate. The winning can be wonderful; that is why people stay in the business. But get your arithmetic wrong, spurred on by masochistic competition, and the losing is painful beyond description.

In the USA, as in Europe, the forces of the market have weeded out the weak or the unlucky; names from the second half of this century are now just footnotes in books. In Europe, a small, fragmented market divided between a surfeit/overabundance of national barriers, the process of rationalisation in the air has been particularly harsh. Indeed, if various governments had not intervened, natural market forces might well have reduced the number of airlines in some countries to a resounding zero.

Those companies which have survived the market's whims and pressures, together with the recent specialist newcomers, have taken on their own distinctive personalities. What their strategies have in common is a feeling that they should not surrender their expertise. 'To grow or not to grow' is all too often a non-existent choice; the main concern is to maintain existing market share. In 1986 the future, for many, looked better and, according to the calculations of a New York stockbroking firm, Stanford C Berstein, the world's airlines in 1984 made operating profits of $3.7 bn. By 1987 it is believed the airlines will reach a peak in operating profits of $17.7 bn and that the subsequent decline will yield profits of $14.5 bn in 1989.

Like all forecasts, the last two figures are based on variables. In air travel the two major variables are GNP growth and changes in ticket pricing. McDonnell Douglas, the well known aircraft manufacturers, use the formula which says revenue passenger miles grow at 1.8 times the rate of GNP. Demand is, however, usually altered by changing fare structures and economic cycles.

A typical situation in which information of this kind can prove invaluable is as follows: Airlines order new aircraft when their existing ones are flying full. If load factors average 65-70% there is often 100% occupancy at peak periods. When planes are full, conditions for the passengers are frequently unbearable. So the airlines must build into their purchasing strategy comfortable passenger conditions without purchasing too much costly extra capacity. The result is a cyclical nightmare of capacity shortages and surpluses not only for the airlines and, incidentally, their passengers, but also the aircraft manufacturers.

Thus strong internal and competitive pressures surround the making of every decision, and the time when the industry was a comfortable one in which to operate are long gone. Many of the strategic problems and options the air industry now faces are the result of its history and the effect it has had on the growth of the modern world. The airlines certainly intensified the 'wind of change' which started with the railways.

Air travel has further shrunk the globe, allowing industrial giants to clone their activities throughout the world and so create universal demands and expectations. Many feel the saturation point for airlines has been reached and, despite the last year's upswing in profits, the picture beyond the 1990s is very unclear.

What Price The Destination?

Since the 1920s we have experienced several changes in objective: from simply reaching destinations and establishing new routes to selling seats and minimising operating costs. We have moved from needing planes for destinations to needing passengers for destinations. The world has been shocked into viewing airline seats as products, part of a package, which need marketing.

The airline chiefs of the world have 'come down to earth', confronted by the same portfolio of problems. Hence the need for strategy. A strategy based on the entrepreneurial use of resources and market information. Every airline needs to take a long, hard look at itself. It is vital to assess strengths and weaknesses honestly, because progress is only assured when it is based on the sum total of unified effort. It cannot and must not come from the charismatic leader who superimposes his will on the rest.

Life for the airlines, as we will repeatedly hear, is not easy. A high degree of sensitivity and an ability to utilise market and competitor knowledge are vital.

For the airline business to survive, professionalism must be of the highest order. Like the other branches of the travel industry, it is both labour and capital intensive and future strategies will have to concentrate on the fact that costs for both are high and the capital difficult to obtain. The capital base must always be sufficient to allow a constant upgrading of the service provided. According to IATA's calculations, an operating profit, before interest, equal to 7.5% of revenues is required to replace international airlines and accommodate the projected growth in traffic. Should this prove impossible then either financing will have to become more imaginative or the number of airlines will get smaller. As state support for national airlines in Europe becomes less, the need for imaginative financial packages will increase. Traditional sources of funds, banks and insurance companies, will probably be superseded by public flotations. In the USA airlines have turned to the public and since 1981 record sums have been raised.

1981 $400m.   1983 $2.4 billion.

The public, however, are growing increasingly discerning and will only invest when they see the airlines sustaining and improving their position. Otherwise, the odds are too high. Everyone in the travel business is clutching a double edged blade; on one side, increasing costs and rivalry and on the other, demanding, and better informed, customers.

Rivalry among existing competitors takes the form of jockeying for position. Unfortunately, the strategic implications of such activity are not always very clear even to the competing companies. Constant rivalry occurs because one or more competitors either feel the pressure or see the opportunity to improve position. There develops a strategy of moves and countermoves which usually benefits neither the initiator nor the copiers and closely resembles the stalemate of trench warfare. We have all seen the disastrous effects of price competition on transatlantic routes and on internal US domestic routes which resulted from this kind of strategic thinking. Originating in the USA, this malaise has infected Europe and could lead to thoughtless price wars. It cannot be repeated often enough: the airlines have to analyse and understand price competition and devise a strategy which gives value added business, rather than temporary bargains.

Reflect on the past. Man has long been fascinated by the air. For centuries it has afforded a special challenge; an opportunity to escape from the confines of everyday life — to travel. Air travel became the ambition of millions and the prestigious flag-carrier of nations. But even in those far off days, nations zealously guarded their air space and international borders. In Europe, within the EEC countries, harmony is now being sought. But the perceptions and the prejudices of the past continue to delay the 'freedom of the skies'. A tragic example of this fanaticism was seen recently when, with a ghastly loss of life, a passenger plane was shot down by fighters for invading Russian air space. Fortunately, there has subsequently been a unique agreement between Russia, USA, and Japan to prevent such a tragedy happening again.

In Europe the European Commission is rather belatedly threatening to haul state-owned airlines to court, to force liberalisation upon them. Naturally, some terrified airlines are frantically lobbying against any form of change. Such action poses an interesting question — why the panic? Upon analysis, the American experience suggests that only the bad airlines need fear deregulation. The well-organised companies — those which have planned for and are geared to effective, competitive strategy, survive and prosper. Eight years after the trauma of deregulation, American airlines have profited from the new system by learning; they have become more innovative and more competitive. Surprisingly, half of the current top American airlines were of little significance when the 1978 deregulation act was passed.

Weaker European airlines should probably consider the strategy of 'Pan Am' and 'Eastern'. Both these companies have staved off bankruptcy by giving their unions company shares and seats on the board in return for wage cuts and freezes. 'Continental' followed a similar pattern when they recently went through technical bankruptcy under Chapter II of American bankruptcy laws. They quickly dismissed about 'two thirds' of the employees in 1983 and halved the payroll for the rest. The result was a doubling of revenue and record profits. What conclusions can we draw from this example? Primarily that productivity within the airlines can be boosted. Most are overmanned. American airline workers are working harder for less money and, unlike Europe, the unions are not in virtual control of the business.

It will be interesting to see how 'B A' will continue to fare in its fight to hold routes and dominate the European airways. The fiercely fought battle for B Cal has cost them dearly.

It still remains comparatively easy to set up an airline company but surviving is a different ballgame. The traditional companies have learned to fight back and the newcomers lack the financial resources to create the necessary hubs, fed by their own networks.

What About Hotels?

Whereas aviation sits very much in the limelight, attracting widespread publicity, another area of the travel industry, hotels, often lacks media appeal. Unless, of course, they manage to 'kill off' vast numbers of their clients through Legionnaire's disease, food poisoning or other hazards!

Throughout the world, over half of all hotel guests are businessmen or conference participants. In relation to revenue this segment produces up to 80% of hotel income. It is therefore hardly surprising that the world hotel chains pay close attention to the needs of the business traveller and how they can be best satisfied.

The Same Problems As The Airlines — Selling The Space

The USA has definitely led the way in the development of modern hotels. The American style has dominated product development and marketing and led to the growth of major look-alike chains across the continents. Hotels have been built in most important locations and the arrival of one hotel chain has usually resulted in the others following close behind. This has led to overcapacity in many corners of the world and a fight to get not 'bottoms on seats' but 'bums on sheets'! Hotels, having once been established, must be filled and therein lies one of the strategic dilemmas of the future.

To date, the major chains, who control more than half of all hotel rooms in the world, have pursued a marketing strategy based on the airlines' approach. This has led to a wide range of product development and the superimposing of a corporate personality and PR image. The main objective is to maintain repeat business: for, according to statistics supplied by the Sheraton, 20% of guests supply 50% of their income. In America reward systems for these treasured clients have been introduced, but in Europe fiscal controls discourage reward programmes for frequent guests.

Recently, a great deal of attention has been paid to analysing client groups and for each identified group hotels have attempted to offer special products and services. Too little time, however, is really spent on monitoring the attrition factor or the effect employees' behaviour has on the prospective guest's image of the hotel. The recent phenomenal worldwide rise in the number of hotels reflects demand, but in the overall strategy of most companies marketing is still being handled far too amateurishly.

Initially, it was an advantage to develop the type of hotels most suitable to different groups; to 'upscale or defrill' according to what the customers wanted. For example, the range runs from the luxury of the Ramada Renaissance-type properties to the Hampton Inn Hotels offering limited-budget deals. The luxury market has even been subdivided into 'luxury budget' and 'luxury'. Obviously, in the latter you get two gold plated taps! It is all based on the theory that your choice of hotel is a reflection of your own self-image or that of your company. This trend has currently led hoteliers to create 'hotels within hotels', in an attempt to be all things to all men. But, despite all this, one is left with the feeling that only lip service is being paid to innovative marketing.

One fascinating and light hearted example of segmentation is the 'love hotels' in Japan. There are 40,000 of these garish, short-stay hotels and their revenues exceed $16 billion per annum, or 1% of GNP. At the moment, as a result of the public morals/business law, they are seeking to modify their image, but this has not stopped them selling their marketing knowledge abroad.

Corporate schemes have evolved to meet the needs of the executive and his company, and better facilities are being developed for women and families on holiday. The focus is very much on profit, but, as Rick Danielson from the Sheraton in his chapter on hotels will point out, the client is the key; and greater efforts must be made to harness the potential within the workforce to provide the type of service the consumer wants and appreciates. The product is not just the bed and the building, but also that intangible something which makes us feel welcome. No matter what area of the travel industry we discuss, it all boils down to the fact that we serve two masters, our shareholders and our customers. Both must be satisfied.

The 1990s will bring even greater specialisation demanding a more complex balancing of costs and profits. Already we see hotels cooperating more and more with other branches, airlines, travel agents and credit card companies. This will increase, as will the mergers, the takeovers and the joint ventures. Networking, embraced so wholeheartedly by small hotels and hotel groups, will continue, and we will observe, too, the development of even more hotels in exotic locations to meet the demand for new and exciting destinations. To achieve success, strategies will have to be based on informed market intelligence, better client feedback, new capital-funding sources and entrepreneurial expertise.

The Importance Of Travel Agents And Tour Operators

Two of the key figures in the balance sheets of airlines and hotels are the tour operator and travel agent. Ever since the days of Thomas Cook, the travel agent and the tour operator have played an increasingly important part in the manufacturing and distribution chain of the travel industry. Their unique role rests in part on their ability to determine the countries in which airlines and hotels need to market their products. Unfortunately, unlike most products, those relating to the travel industry are intangible, subject to international fluctuations in supply and demand, difficult to brand and rather expensive. On top of this, the product very often exists in another country and is not under the direct control of the distributor.

In fact, it is not always very clear what the product is. It is definitely not just the destination. Indeed many people are indifferent to their destination due to the ease with which 'sunny Greece, Spain, Italy or Malta', can be substituted one for the other. One consequence of this has been the emergence of a definite, consistent product — the packaging of a sundrenched dream. Thus companies like Thomas Cook (UK owned) and Woodside Management Systems (US owned) are faced with the necessary task of marketing their own services, creating client awareness and providing a care-orientated service programme for their customers, while at the same time distributing the products of other companies.

Achieving these objectives usually means, for both the tour operator and travel agent, huge outlays on advertising, PR systems and worldwide representation. Most leisure travel abroad is controlled by agents and operators, because the majority of people lack the time, experience or knowledge to help themselves. A holiday, rather like a business trip abroad, can be best termed as a 'high advice product'. Low advice products, such as simple ticket transactions, timings and pricings, can be supplied via technology, but the actual emotional involvement which the public requires, when buying a trip, can only come via face to face contact. Technology can be used to give more information, for example, by videos. It can speed up systems, improve communications and provide data bases for further selling. But the travel agent and tour operator, in person, will always be the travellers' dream merchant.

To predict the future can be dangerous, yet key trends are so dominant that one can confidently forecast a greater concentration of travel agents and tour operators in the market. The larger agencies will continue to account for increasingly larger shares of the business and we will see, particularly on the tour-operating side, other sectors of the industry encroaching more and more on their activities. British Airways, for example, recently declared its intention of building up its package tour interests to match those of UK market leaders Thomson and Intasun. Thomas Cook, too, is now offering its own holidays.

Tour operators seek each season to create not only demand but also loyalty. The tactics used are aggressive; brochures appear earlier and earlier, and the special offers become more diverse and often borderline in their value.

A recent promotional activity involved a major charity benefitting from sales. No doubt, we will see more of the same in the attempts by the giants Thomsons and Intasun to increase their market share.

There is no doubt tour operators buy market share, and that as far as holidays are concerned the public are notoriously fickle. The main thrust is geared at getting people to book as early as possible. In 1988 however, the early sale of package holidays has been disappointing.

The fight to place 'packaged' tourists on foreign soil is on and, as the giant planes disgorge their human cargo, the tour operators and travel agents are in danger of creating an emotional distance between themselves and their customers. The whole process is in danger of becoming so painstakingly planned, costed and rationalised, that it passes beyond the point of acceptability and becomes remote. Operating margins are low, price cutting continuous and we are seeing the tour operator being placed under more and more pressure.

The travel agents have a distinct advantage over the tour operators for they can rely on revenue stemming from two major sources rather than just one: namely, the leisure and business market.

The travel business could be heading in the area of air travel ticketing into stormy weather. A minor hurricane is brewing over the IATA plan to offer bigger commissions (up to 15%) to so called "super agents". "Super agents" are those who invest heavily in automation and marketing and so take more of the eager to state that they are not trying to split the association's 50,000 agency members round the world into two tiers. But travel agents, already conscious of other possible changes threatening their livelihoods, are sceptical.

Today travel agents sell three out of four tickets bought by air travellers. This could be changing. Since airlines were deregulated in America eight years ago, they have been free to experiment with new ways of selling tickets. This now is reaching cartelised Europe and we will see increasing evidence of

* automated ticketing machines via credit cards
* entry of mail order firms and supermarkets into ticketing

* availability of electronic data base publications via teletext which could allow their publishers — ABC World Airways Guide and the Official Airline Guides — to become airticket retailers too
* perhaps the most threatening, for European travel agents, is the way some companies, with large business travel accounts, are threatening to take up ticket writing activities themselves. The cost of this venture would be covered by the commissions collected, which would normally go to the travel agent.

Happily, the business travel sector growth pattern is virtually assured and will possibly outstrip economic and trade growth figures by the end of the century.

The battle for business accounts is under way. It is a battle in which the small travel agents cannot seek to compete. First, because they cannot match the discounts offered by the large scale companies. Second, because they often cannot cope with the capital investment required to obtain business accounts and then maintain them.

The large travel agents are focusing more and more on exploiting the new service of expenses-management. American Express, through its computer based Travel Management System, offers a comprehensive, centralised system to manage each and every phase of corporate travel. It has been developed as a result of an intermarriage between the corporate card, which is the payment system, and the business travel service. A key segment has been identified in the USA, to whom this service will be targeted; namely the top Fortune 150 corporations, half of which use the card. Its objective is to manage every stage of the business travel cycle, from planning through to reconciliation and review. There are many critics of such a system and, naturally, rivals are emerging; the major one being the World Travel Service Programme supported by Citicorp, Diners' Club, and the Universal Federation of Travel Agents Association. Under the scheme — pioneered in Britain, and to be introduced initially in the UK, West Germany, France, US, and Australia — customers will be offered a range of services co-ordinated through Citicorp and Diners' Club.

The underlying strength of the scheme is not just the customer data base, but also the World Travel Vouchers. The World Travel Voucher is a universally acceptable, standard piece of paper which will be bankable by hotels and, shortly, car rental companies. This will replace existing agency vouchers which hotels have to present to the originating agency for payment. Participating agencies will also offer business customers corporate Diners' Club cards and Citicorp travellers cheques. It will be interesting to see how things develop.

A recent survey conducted in the UK by the Business Traveller Magazine showed that the company card market was split as follows:

American Express — 30%

Diners' Club — 16%

Obviously, Diners', now safely under the wing of the mighty Citicorp, will be eager to fight back to obtain the lion's share of the remaining 44%.

The message from the credit card companies is that firms can eliminate cash floats by the use of corporate cards. Intriguingly it is a popular message with British firms. They appear to have adopted this system more readily than the Americans. Some 64% of UK companies use credit cards in some form, compared with 55% of similar USA organisations. The further adoption of this system will mean that fewer companies will provide temporary cash advances to employees for travel and accommodation purposes. This means the agencies involved in business travel will bear the cost. Only the large companies will be able to finance and operate such a service without major cash flow problems.

How Do You Compete?

How then, can small travel agencies compete with the warring giants?

The solution could lie in the formation of groupings of independents, rather like the approach recently adopted by smaller hotels. In the USA groupings like this have been established, taking on the form of franchise operations, licensing deals, marketing groups and so on. Technology provides these groups with easy access to data bases and efficient distribution and communication systems. By joining together, erstwhile independent agencies are able to use effectively economies of scale and enjoy increased purchasing power. Two of the major groupings in the USA are Woodside Management Systems and Travel Trust International.

This type of approach could be exploited effectively in Europe because it brings major benefits in the form of lower prices (through volume purchase) more sophisticated marketing techniques, greater sensitivity to the market place and wider sales opportunities. Networking in this form could provide European markets with a reliable second and third tier of travel suppliers, thus maintaining a wider choice range. As a system it is difficult to establish and, because of the different companies involved, prone to many operating and management difficulties. However, Woodside, the major example in the USA, already has overseas members, amongst which are leading agencies such as Hogg Robinson, Hapag Lloyd and Voyage Wirtz.

Woodside supplies an ongoing, dynamic service which is constantly evolving and diversifying. Its latest sophisticated reservations system, ARMS, is capable of translating all the different suppliers' reservations systems and then processing them into its own system. This means all reservations worldwide are simultaneously processed by one computer, giving instant replies. This development brings a truly global aspect to what was once a purely American operation, enabling Woodside to outstrip major rivals who are dependent on each supplier's systems for their reservations. Naturally, the competitive advantage will be lost as similar systems are quickly introduced, but Woodside is conscious of the price/ service combination and will continue to bring satisfaction to its clients by giving a centralised, yet local, service through the universally high standards of their members.

Technology — The Answer?

In the fight for market shares, tour operators and travel agents will seek to use technology more effectively. Information systems offering search procedures, data bases, integrated text and image will become more widely used. Office systems will become even more acceptable to employees and will help streamline communications, records, office management and billing procedures. The public will become more directly linked with the distributors and manufacturers through videotext and, as digital chips replace some 400 analogue television components in the family T.V., a new horizon of advertising and promotional opportunities will open up. The industrialised, T.V.-owning world will then be provided with a residential information infrastructure in the same way that the telephone system provides it with a communications infrastructure. The cost of computer logic and memory is continually declining due to the competitive nature of the business and this, combined with increased familiarity, will gradually result in a better understanding of the actual potential a computer has. Unfortunately, to date, most home-used computers have been lost in a *cul de sac* of arcade games.

So far as the travel industry is concerned, the impact of this development on Europe's marketing and advertising boundaries will be tremendous, particularly when coupled with cable T.V. The pan-European channel 'Sky Channel' now has 3.6 million subscribers, mostly in Holland, but by the end of 1985 the European audience is expected to be over 7 million. The British ITV network also plans a 'Superchannel', which will eventually broadcast, with advertising breaks, for 18 hours a day to the whole of Europe.

The possibilities are limitless, and the winners will be the companies best able to take advantage of these new developments. Unfortunately, too many companies are locked into a structure which is wholly inadequate for the future.

What Role Should The Tour Operator Play?

Over the years, tour operators have divided into those dealing with the masses, and the small, very specialised companies. Like hotels, the major operators are attempting to be all things to all men, seeking to dominate the market by satisfying all identified segments. This is a difficult strategy to follow and one which requires expert handling and control. Company strategy must be constantly updated in response to a continuing appraisal of customers' needs if such handling and control are to be developed. After all, companies are not just there to provide packages and services but also to cater for the needs of the customers.

In the future, there will be an increasing need for joint ventures and cooperations, together with a trend towards networking in distribution outlets, using such outlets as banks and insurance companies. Many of the large companies make no secret of their plans to diversify and it is becoming an important part of their strategy. In the case of joint ventures, operators will benefit from combined experience and extra funding. The recent cooperation between Bass and Horizon on overseas holiday projects resulted in Horizon receiving £12.2 million from Bass for 15% of Horizon stock.

As far as the holiday-maker is concerned, increased time will be spent on designing more exotic or sporting holidays; and there will be an increased need to choose hotels on a qualitative as well as a quantitative basis. (This point applies particularly to UK companies, for their counterparts on the continent often provide much higher standards.) Changing social habits and improving life styles will have to be taken into account. For the vast majority of holiday makers, travel has not necessarily broadened the mind: in fact, it has done much to strengthen myths and prejudices. Perhaps part of the role of the future tour operator will be to encourage the understanding of people by avoiding nationality-dominated hotels and centres. Club Mediterranean has provided just such a melting pot for different races, and its success speaks for itself; it has been a demonstration of imagination and anticipation.

In the future, the tour operator will have to pay considerably more attention to its brochures. The brochure is, to all intents and purposes, the 'product' and there is no way the travel agent can modify this product, once printed. There should, therefore, be greater cooperation between tour operator, travel agent and hotelier to provide much more distinctive brochures which enable customers to distinguish between the various 'products' on offer. Improved quality does not necessarily mean extra costs, in fact brochures could contain some form of advertising — swimwear and sports goods, banking and insurance — to make the publication more self-supporting. The travel agent's premises is there to attract customers and therefore the effective distribution of a well designed, accessible and comprehensible brochure becomes a major marketing aim.

Conclusions

In this volatile market, tour operators will survive and prosper, not by taking part in price wars, but by developing a more efficient marketing management strategy, orientated towards clearly defined objectives. Previous assessments of the market were too simple and failed to reflect adequately the more complex needs of today's customers. Future product-packages must be more flexible and better presented if they are to display effectively what the package offers the customer.

What Price Insurance?

Insurance for the businessman and the holiday-maker is essential — offering protection against minor and, sometimes, more dramatic events. However, the needs of these two main segments of the travel industry are different. For the holiday-maker, the loss of a suitcase is usually just a minor inconvenience. But for the businessman the loss of clothes, documents, and samples can be disastrous.

Travel insurance policies, as we all know, vary considerably in style, content and benefits. The friendly grin of the insurance man when he collects the premium can all too often change into a shrug of the shoulders and a shake of the head when a claim is registered. The majority of policies appear to cover all eventualities and those of us who purchase airline tickets via Amex or Diners' usually receive a form of package cover automatically. This type of cover, useful as it is, does not, however, indemnify against specific risks, and thus requires some form of topping up. Some insurance companies have attempted to fill the gap by offering specially-designed, annual insurance policies to the frequent traveller. In an attempt to obtain company travel policies, insurance companies discount the premium when large numbers are insured.

Not surprisingly, flexible cover is expensive and, unfortunately, too many companies offer outdated policies. The risks attached to travel are enormous, and the policy contained in the back of the holiday brochure, convenient though it is, does not necessarily meet all needs. Why, then, is everybody in the business so eager to sell insurance cover to travellers? The answer is simple — profits and commission. Let us remember that 3,343 million people travel worldwide each year. If only half buy insurance, the turnover involved for insurance companies and intermediaries is colossal. In fact, for those tour operators who operate on very narrow profit margins, the fees earned from travel insurance brokerage are crucial to the financial well-being of the company. So, in actual fact, the insurance payments contribute to the overall financial viability of the company, be it Thomsons, Pan America or whoever. At the moment, this business is being handled in a very amateurish way, particularly by travel agents and travel operators. But it is hoped that, in the future, this will change and a much more professional service will be offered to the consumer.

The standard of advice on insurance given by the travel agent and tour operators' organisation is very poor, and in-house insurance forms are usually advised, regardless of whether they fit or meet the individual's needs.

The Future — How Will We Get There?

Distinct divisions between the different branches of our industry will vanish, for the major participants will amalgamate the various roles of carrier, tour operator, hotelier and so forth, in an integrated operation. At the same time, however, we will see a greater spread of niche specialisation and management groups. The former will usually be the innovators for the industry, and the latter will help huge conglomerates control their empires, providing the specialised services required. The involvement of ancillary industries will continue and could, given the increasing complexities of technological application and the need for capital, lead to the travel industry being absorbed by mighty sleeping giants like IBM.

The future will be exciting, but the going will be rough. Many will fall by the wayside, their names disappearing by the 1990s.

Economic and social instability will be our backcloth, and only in those organisations where each department and individual works to a common, clearly-defined, strategic goal, will success be possible. We all know how to do things better. But, sadly, it often just doesn't happen. We are all captives of outdated systems, locked into everyday operating problems. We must force ourselves to look to the future, and the way ahead should be clear:

— technology — buy wisely, use to advantage
— be cost efficient — share developments, share costs
— identify and exploit across markets
— understand your organisation and its needs.

Adèle Hodgson is currently a consultant in Brussels with Global Partners, a company specialising in the financial and travel industries. Over the past few years her activities have included developing marketing strategies in major companies, lecturing and writing articles.

2

Railways

What Happens When The Rug Is Pulled Out?

We all claim that our own industry is unique. The railways industry may have more of a right to make this claim than most. Railways have always been uniquely closed systems running their own vehicles on their own track, calling at their own terminals, operating their own sales outlets. Not only do they own and operate these massive undertakings, but many of them design and build their own vehicles and infrastructure, as well as maintain them.

As if this were not enough to manage, some own bus companies, hotel chains, shipping and ferry companies and other diverse, but usually travel-related, activities. Within the travel industry it is hard to think of other activities or organisations so insulated from the outside world and with such a propensity for introversion.

Railways have another, unique, edge. In most countries governments have granted a monopoly to one organisation to run the railway system in that country. Granted, this is not a monopoly on all transport; but, on the assumption that this particular mode of transport has some very real advantages, this should put each national operator in a pretty competitive position with substantial profit opportunities. The average European railway has an asset base equivalent to a large manufacturing company, revenues larger than many well known European store groups and market shares in principal markets which would attract anti-trust actions in other trading situations.

So What Is The Average Profitability Like?

Profitability is appalling. On average, Europe's principal railways made trading losses for each of the last five years and not because of social obligations or heavy investment.

Since the early 1970s when the Common Market Commission tried to get to grips with railway finances and devised the system of Public Service

Obligation (PSO) payments which Common Market members could pay to railway companies to run services for social reasons, there have been clearly defined contract payments from local and central authorities and these are included as legitimate customer revenues. But despite these enormous contract sums, which are awarded without competitive tender, all the European railway companies managed to lose money over the last five years and this is before paying interest on loans and allowing for reinvestment needs.

This Poses Some Interesting Questions

- Are railway cost structures inherently uncompetitive against other modes?
- Are they badly managed?
- Do they suffer from state interference in normal commercial decision making?
- Are the travel products marketed by railways unattractive compared to competitive travel products and compared to all the other products and services competing for the consumer's discretionary spending power?

The answer is a combination of all these things.

Railways are old technology. By 1852 Britain's mainline system was complete and by 1914 so were the railway systems of the rest of the industrial world.

During this period railways dominated the economic development of Europe. Apart from their vital role in the movement of freight and creation of industry and their strategic role in the event of military conflict, railways created mass consumer markets and, in creating them, monopolised them.

Governments could clearly not allow activities so fundamental to the economic and social fabric of their countries to act in a free market way. Initially the railway companies were enormously powerful and governments acted in a regulatory role preventing the abuses of monopoly power. The massive capital investments needed to create railways were not always well managed and the knock-on effect of bankruptcies, particularly in the railway mania years of the 1800s, had serious economic and political effects and so, again, governments became involved.

So dependent did western nations become on the travel and transport infrastructures created by railways that governments could not allow these structures to disappear when railway companies became unable to manage them on an economic basis. Thus state involvement shifted from regulation of excess to protection of weakness and a combination of these elements exists in most of the regulatory frameworks surrounding railways today.

The effect of this involvement on the railway organisations themselves has, on the whole, been bad. This has been the case since the 1950s when new travel and transport technologies, developed earlier in the century but prevented from expanding in consumer markets by two world wars, came into their own. For consumer travel markets the fifties and sixties were the age of the car and the seventies and eighties, the age of the plane.

Railway market shares dropped dramatically in rapidly expanding markets and the regulatory environment in which railway organisations by then existed worked directly against any effective competitive response. Railway managements were no longer running commercial organisations. For many years they had been running public utilities which, like health, water, power, etc., were designated 'good things' which the state should provide. Exactly what social worth railway organisations provided through their transport and travel services was no more easy to define than any other social service. Railways were being driven by the need to fit into the role of an instrument of government policy, with all its paraphernalia of political decision-making and often spurious cost/benefit measurement, and, at the same time, by an obsession with the operation of the railway system itself.

What they were not driven by was the market and meeting customer needs. Railway managements became over-dominated by engineers and transport econometricians. So they missed out.

So Where Are We Now?

The above scenario is pretty dismal and one might expect the present and the future to be equally gloomy. But perhaps not so. Whilst it is not yet easy to spot in the statistics of market share or ROI, there are indications that railways are poised for a significant comeback. Why is this?

Conventional wisdom identifies the oil crises of the mid and late seventies as the cause. However the link is often simplistic. At the time of the O.P.E.C. price hikes there was a scramble for solutions and alternative policies, and railways were identified not only as being fuel efficient (that rather depended on how you did your sums) but more usefully as potential consumers of secondary energy sources, viz., electricity, the generation of which was not dependent on any one primary energy source and, in particular, could be independent of oil.

There is no doubt that such thinking did lead to the commencement of a number of major new railway projects, the most spectacular of which was the French TGV. However, the flaw in identifying this as the prime mover in the re-emergence of railways is that the oil crises did not last.

Other sources of oil came on stream, total western demand dropped and competitive transport modes improved their fuel efficiency considerably. Who talks now about railways as the fuel efficient travel mode of the future?

Fɪɢ. 2.1. The highly successful 160 mph French TGV.

Much more significant was the effect of the oil crises on the economies of European countries. For the first time since the end of the war they felt poor.

The effect has been twofold.

The first, and most obvious, is that governments have less money to spend. Not only that, but many social welfare programmes have become so entrenched that governments are obliged to fund them, leaving the area for discretionary cost savings to take an even bigger burden of economy than might otherwise be the case. The second is a socio/political effect which has caused a shift to the political right in virtually all the western democracies. The combined effect of these two changes has been to make less money available for subsidising railways at the same time as a decline in the political and social will to spend such money anyway.

Can this be good news?

Yes, if it means that in order to survive, railways have to adapt. Fortunately, in most countries, an orgy of cost cutting and retrenchment has not followed. There have been before, too many years of this for anyone to believe that it will do other than decimate the systems. And, strangely, railways seem to generate a love/hate relationship between themselves and their publics: whilst the disenchantment with further subsidisation has grown it has been combined with a great reluctance to see the railway systems disappear.

The solution, therefore, has to be in the re-emergence of commercially viable railway systems and this can only be achieved by the emergence of commercially oriented management with radically new strategies.

It is the sporadic evidence of just such changes in railway management cultures that provides the basis for believing that British Rail's advertising may have been right, if perhaps a little premature, in claiming that this was (about to be) The Age of the Train.

These management changes are not coming easily. Some are being generated from within the organisations themselves, as in the case of British Rail's sector management concept, whereas others are being imposed, as in the case of the appointment of an ex IBM manager to head up the Deutsche Bundesbahn. But in each case the objective is the same: to move the organisations away from their historic roles as state suppliers of commodity transport to much more conventional roles as commercial organisations, motivated more by profit than social purpose, rather leaving the latter to government to decide, but being more than pleased to act as contractors if so required, and if sufficiently rewarded.

Fortunately most European railways are well placed to make this transition into the real world. The dominance of engineers in recent decades has at least left a legacy of good infrastructure and, in many cases, good vehicles to run on it. The new European railway managers are not faced with the appalling track standards of many North American railway systems which make the creation of competitive rail products almost impossible without massive reinvestment.

But it is clear that the real pressure causing change in railway systems throughout the developed world is not strategic but financial. Governments are just not prepared to carry on subsidising, at enormous cost, transport systems which often deliver poor and expensive products and for which, in very many instances, there are better and cheaper alternatives.

Fortunately this tide in the affairs of railways coincides nicely with some useful shifts in the travel market place. The two principal competitive modes of private car and plane have now passed the peak of their intangible product benefits. There is little novelty or emotional utility now in either of these modes and yet their original growth phases were charged with the benefits of freedom, status and excitement. Now their very success has brought with is the negatives of congestion, lack of exclusivity and over-familiarity. On the domestic travel front there has been little significant product innovation in the last 30 years and even air travel has seen little more than cosmetic changes since the explosion in overseas holidays in the seventies.

So the time is ripe for a relaunch of a mode of transport which many consumers have not experienced for years. But it will not happen by itself; and the existing railway organisations, in which the development of a new management approach is still a delicate bloom, may yet fudge it.

This chapter is devoted to helping them make the most of the best opportunity they are ever likely to get.

In Search Of A Strategy

The financial turnarounds that the passenger railways of the world will have to make even to approach financial viability are not going to be achieved by doing the same things better. They are going to need completely new strategies.

But railway planning departments have been producing strategies for years, with little noticeable effect. The need now for each railway company is for a new corporate strategy which permeates right through its entire organisation.

For this to happen, the strategy must be capable of being encapsulated in a corporate philosophy, in a corporate statement and mission which everyone can understand and to which everyone can work. Many railways currently have such cultures, but they are invariably oriented towards operations, safety, or engineering. Our new corporate missions must be totally commercially oriented, whilst building on the enormous tangible and intangible strengths which railways have evolved over the years.

Let us explore the creation of a series of such statements and see what sort of strategic options emerge.

Statement 1 'To operate the best (in terms of customer estimates of product quality) and most profitable transport and travel company in Europe.'

As a corporate statement, this directs us away from thinking of ourselves as a railway company, and consequently something special, towards being one of the many companies in the travel and transport business. And it combines an objective of financial viability with a customer orientation which will both assist in achieving that viability and also support any continuing social role.

Let us take our thinking a little further. Our next step is to re-orientate our attitudes towards the hardware. We must forget railways as any special organisation or transport system, and just think of trains as our unbeatable way of offering the best transport and travel products to the market place.

Statement 2 'We use trains to create the best transport and travel products available.'

So far we've talked about total railway organisations, but this book is really only about the passenger travel industry. Many railway companies see freight as the bedrock of their operation with passenger travel as a secondary, marginal, activity. But this is just a question of shared costs and customer definition. From now on we'll deal only with the passenger travel market, although the principles established may have just as much relevance to the freight businesses. Our next step, then, is to segment this market for the movement of people.

Perhaps the first and, for railway organisations, the most important segmentation is to identify those parts of the market where the consumer himself is the primary customer and those where first purchasing decisions are made by government, be it local or central.

Statement 3 'We sell travel products to either individual consumers or central or local government.'

The Government As Customer

Positioning the state as just another customer, albeit a fairly important one, is useful in separating that role of government from its other, very different, roles as principal shareholder and banker of its national railway company. It is important because the continuation of the first relationship is in no way conditional on the maintenance of the other two. It also enables us to be completely customer-oriented in all aspects of our business and therefore to create a market-based strategy from which all other, e.g., engineering, personnel and labour relations, operating and finance, can follow.

Our statement said that we sell travel products to government. That is true, but we should also note that government buys travel products in an unfinished form. Basically it pays for the provision of travel facilities in certain places and under certain circumstances by funding the infrastructure, facilitating hardware, i.e., vehicles, and in some cases a proportion of variable costs. It may specify a basic level of consumer product which must be provided but, having done this and paid for it, it then commissions the same railway organisation which has supplied the facilities to take this basic product and market it to the end consumer in various forms; either at market-based prices which, in themselves, would be insufficient to cover the full costs of providing the particular travel products, or at lower prices specified by government for its own reasons.

It is far better to position the relationship with the state as a customer in this way rather than the more traditional view of the railway organisation failing to make ends meet and being subsidised. The PSO system is supposed to do just this but political rhetoric and often the pronouncements of railway organisations themselves show that the concept is only skin deep — a mere window dressing of the subsidised public service orientation which went before. Yet it is vitally important to the new breed of railway managers that it is seen in this way. The analogy is best drawn with contract caterers. They do not see themselves as lame ducks receiving financial support from the various corporations for which they provide employee food services. Rather they perceive themselves as sharp commercial operators competing for valuable contracts which will earn them profits.

Nor do they overly concern themselves with the reasons why their corporate customers want to provide below-cost meals. This is not to say that they do not fully understand the motivations of their customers; but this understanding enables them to meet the needs of these customers and to fend off competition, now and in the future. The important thing is that they do not need to share in these motivations. Exactly the same positioning is required by railway companies when they act as contract suppliers to government. A deep understanding of the needs of their state customers but not a sharing in them. To gain this understanding let us look at the reasons why governments pay such large PSO sums for the provision of train services. Social need would appear to be the principal reason. The very title Public Service Obligation payment suggests it. But does this stand up to investigation?

Travel tends to be a relatively up-market activity and train travellers in particular tend to be in the higher socio economic groups, not the sort of people usually requiring state assistance. In many cases, the provision of state funded assistance with artificially low consumer prices has generated consumer behaviour which now requires the maintenance of these low prices to continue with an acceptable equilibrium.

This is particularly so in the case of commuter services into and out of large cities. Artificially low prices have caused a movement of population out of the suburbs and into the surrounding towns and villages where property prices have risen to balance the low travel cost with city centre earning potential. Few would describe the average commuter as socially disadvantaged and in need of state support, but state support he gets and in massive quantity. The Catch 22 is that the commuter, having made personal financial decisions based on the artificially low level of commuter fares now genuinely cannot afford to pay any more. Government policies not to increase the level of these fares are, therefore, based much more on the political reality of negative electorate reaction than on any real social need.

Even where governments pay for the provision of travel facilities to and from isolated rural communities, there is little good evidence that such social services are best provided by train travel. The continuation of such services is, therefore, again primarily for political need rather than for any true social purpose.

There are, of course, other possible reasons for maintaining a national railway system. Economic and environmental considerations are often quoted, but these have more to do with the freight businesses than passenger travel; and the once vital military consideration is now of much less significance and not seriously proposed as a reason for maintaining rail systems over and above any other form of transport.

So it would appear that the underlying reason for state support of train travel services is not social, economic, environmental or strategic but political. When it comes to the crunch there are votes to be lost from cutting out train services or significantly raising certain train fares.

However, having identified this prime motivation for state support of train travel, there is no suggestion that this reason is bad, partly because this, in itself, would be a political judgment but, much more importantly, because our new breed of railway managers should not be second guessing government policies but rather thoroughly understanding their implication for the future success of their business.

And what is the implication of a primarily political basis for the government contracting for the provision of train services? Probably one of risk. Such a basis for decision-making must be inherently unstable, and history has shown it to be so. The message for our new strategy must, therefore, be one of risk reduction. We will return to this later.

The Consumer As Customer

For all the importance of central and local government as customers for train travel services, they are not the consumers of them.

Rail travel products are, at the end of the day, consumed by individual customers, generally acting independently and going through exactly the same sort of purchase decisions as they do for all the other many goods and services that they consume every day of the week.

So we need a marketing strategy for our customers.

Statement 4 'We segment our customers and identify their different needs. We design profitable products to meet these needs.'

It is worth noting that this statement applies equally well to government customers as travel contracts are usually divided between central and local government and there is often considerable disparity between their various objectives and motivations. The more up-to-date railway companies are reasonably familiar with market segmentation. Concepts of short and long distance travellers; business, commuting and leisure travellers; high price and low price travellers are to be found in many passenger marketing activities. However, the application of such segmentation is often very limited.

One of the problems which has bedevilled railways is the relative ease with which they can be economically modelled. No good econometric modeller would claim that his models are anything more than an approximation of the real world but, unfortunately, within railway planning departments they have been taken much further than this and have led to the simplistic notion of an almost undifferentiated railway product, i.e., the basic train service, but a differentiated market which has varying levels of propensity to pay.

This had led to the awful concept of the fares structure and its associated communication problems. Our statement said that after having segmented customers into different groups we 'identify their different needs and then design profitable products to meet these needs'. This statement is market-oriented, the concept of fares structure is system-led.

The need for careful segmentation will grow as consumer markets move away from the mass markets of the middle part of the 20th century into more and more varying needs and aspirations. Many of the old groupings are no longer relevant as spending power becomes much more equally spread amongst socio economic groups and where many consumers have achieved all their tangible product needs and search for intangible benefits and opportunities for self-expression.

Such moves are now clearly apparent in almost all other consumer markets on a world-wide basis and have profound implications for product design, product life cycles and communication strategies. It is absolutely vital for railway companies to move away from the commodity view of their own services which currently predominates and into 'lifestyle' products relevant to today's and tomorrow's consumers.

Designing The Product Range

What are the range of products that a railway company, like any other service company, has to offer to its customers? As they are designed for customers it is best to approach them from a customer viewpoint.

A customer wishes to buy something (or a number of things) from the rail company. To make such a purchase decision he must have a fairly clear picture of what he expects to receive and, in return, is prepared to pay for it. With this approach it is easy to see that a journey from A to B is a product. But that product could have been purchased from a bus company or an airline, or the same consumer end-benefit achieved by the customer driving his car.

How does the customer choose between these competing alternatives? Quite easily, because each of the products on offer is not just the commodity journey from A to B but a whole bundle of tangible and intangible attributes, all of which influence the customer's choice. When a customer buys a Saver ticket from British Rail to travel between Manchester and London he buys the following:

— the ability to be in London rather than Manchester;
— on a certain day;
— for the journey to take a certain time;
— for his choice of journeys to be limited to off-peak times;
— a degree of comfort;
— the availability of a whole range of ancillary products such as car parking, food service, telephones, newspapers, feeder services at terminals;

— to be in the standard (2nd class) rather than deluxe (1st class) accommodation;
— a certain ambience from the presence of other customers;
— a degree of safety, high in some aspects, lower in others;
— plenty of space to move about;
— no videos;
— the ability to buy a meal on the train;
— little staff contact;
— some inconvenience with luggage;
— the need to get from the station to his final destination;
— the ability to return to Manchester in the same way within one month;
— the pleasure associated with his journey purpose;
— the pleasant associations of train travel from previous experiences.

and for all these things, and many others, he is prepared to pay £22.

From this definition the product is clearly not the InterCity train or Customer Service, or the station. The consumer can buy none of these. They are merely attributes, albeit important ones, of the total product which the customer defined when he asked for a Saver to London and put £22 on the counter. The same applies to First Class, Pullman and Second Standard. Season tickets are the equivalent of bulk packs in food marketing.

But is this not just the fares structure? Of course it is, but the evolution of differential fares and the need for mechanisms to prevent trading down has led to the accidental development of a number of different products on sale at different prices — a product range. The market has forced railway companies into what they should have been doing anyway and a realisation of this and a consequent reorientation away from the concept of fares structure brings considerable benefits.

First, the benefit of ease of communication. All travel companies worry over the complexity of their fares structure and consumers' inability to comprehend it. Customers are just not interested in fares structures. Each different customer wishes to know which travel products are appropriate for him and no more.

Individual product design, which includes advertising, design, media choice, packaging and pricing will direct customers to the appropriate products for them and avoid any need for understanding of the whole range. It is not necessary to understand a car manufacturer's total product range to select the right car for yourself. In this way more products can be produced for more market segments, which will increase profitability rather than simplifying fare structures, which will sub-optimise and reduce profits.

The concept of product range and product design leads also to the concept of product management. Railway companies, with their production orientation, are in exactly the same position as consumer goods manufacturers in the early sixties when management was by production line and the sales force existed to shift the results of an optimum production effort out of the warehouse to make room for more. The introduction of product management was so enormously successful that all companies moved over to it in a short space of years.

There is no better way of ensuring that each of a company's products is in tune with ever-changing customer needs and ever-changing competition and yet few travel companies have so far adopted it. Management is still by geographic area or by production line, i.e., route. It is organised for ease of administration and to manage assets not in line with the market.

The idea of product design to satisfy customer wants is also very important in the state contract areas, both to maximise revenues from this source and to provide the consumer franchise necessary to support the contracts. National and local authority customers look for very different benefits from those that consumers do, although satisfying these requirements is often achieved through the same product features. The need to recognise this in the design of the product range is of great importance in the areas where state contracts are sought.

However, it should not only be customer requirements which are part of product design — profitability must be built in too. Far too many railway staff are employed on fraud prevention and this generates a culture where all customers are perceived as potential criminals. With profitability designed in, customer contact personnel can work hard, confident in the knowledge that the more they do for the customer the more they do for their company.

Discretionary Effort

When we listed the Saver product attributes, the list was long on tangible benefits but rather short on intangibles. Yet in many products and markets it is the intangibles which give the greatest product differentiations and the greatest consumer motivations. This is particularly so in service industries like travel. Yet the personnel policies in most railway companies follow the pattern of manufacturing industry, where an accurate measure of labour input and product output is possible. In services the difference between a good product and a mediocre one is the amount of discretionary effort which staff use in their delivery of the product to the customer.

The very rigid industrial relations of railway companies work directly against the generation of any such discretionary effort and yet this is the area where enormous product improvements can be achieved. There is a recognition of the need for something better here which manifests itself in the proliferation of Customer Service programmes now visible in many travel companies, but many of these programmes are flawed in that they treat the symptoms and not the structural cause and because they are often separated from normal business management and product design.

Different travel products require different levels of customer service, and therefore of discretionary effort, and such intangible benefits must be built into the product specification from the outset and not treated as some nice warm overlay which blankets everything the organisation does.

However, building them into the production specification will be difficult for most companies as, without a recognition of the concept of product and product management, they are unlikely to have created product specifications. Such a situation would be unthinkable in a manufacturing company for, without a product specification, how does production know what to produce and how can you maintain quality control? The answer, of course, is that they do not and you cannot.

This situation is all too apparent when one looks at many rail products and leads quickly to the Gronroos syndrome where production management cuts cost, which affects product quality, which reduces revenue, which puts further pressure on costs.

Production managers are not supposed to have to guess at what level of service has been costed into which products to be sold, and at what price. They need product specifications which are prepared by product managers to achieve a profitable product design for an identified market segment.

Product Profitability

One of the reasons why railway management is asset-oriented rather than market-oriented is because of the perceived difficulties in measuring product profitability. So many costs have, over the years, been lumped together that the best that is achieved in many organisations is simple revenue per kilometre figures and maybe some abstraction/generation calculations. Even this latter, elementary, exercise is not always carried out and many companies work on the basis that all revenue is incremental and contributes in full to the fixed costs of the system and that these costs are equal for all products.

Nothing could be further from the truth.

In fairness it should be noted that a number of railways have recognised the need to measure profit at much lower levels than previously and work hard at identifying costs with activities. However, the models which are arising would be, to use the manufacturing industry analogy again, like measuring profit by production line. Certainly measures such as asset yield and productivity are important but as most of the management variables which affect profit are product based, e.g. price, specification and volume, then production line profitability is of limited use. We must have product profit.

SNCF and BR seem to have made the biggest steps in this direction. Both have been using sophisticated market research surveys for some years to assess the abstraction or cannibalisation of any new product from existing ones. Both have also been careful to identify the direct costs of marketing and administration, although there is still much room for improvement here.

Perhaps the biggest step that they have both taken is to abandon the notion that everything new can be marginally costed and to seek to calculate generated train costs by product. This has led to some interesting results. The difference between peak and off-peak train costs is considerable, and products which only generate off-peak costs can be much more profitable than those with higher unit revenues but which incur higher peak time costs. Differences in capacity utilisation between First and Second Class, partly due to lower seat densities and partly due to peaky First Class demand, give much higher unit costing for First Class and make the previously desirable high unit revenues look a lot less acceptable. To date the models for such costing have been simple. SNCF have used their red, white and blue days as the basis for different costs and BR's operational research department have produced figures for peak and off-peak for each of the three passenger sectors of InterCity, London and South East and Provincial.

That so many of the costs in railway systems appear to be shared has a lot more to do with management decisions in the past than the inherent structure of railways. The historic production orientation created an obsession with cost reduction which led to the centralisation of many functions and attempted optimisation of resources through intensive and shared use. It is questionable now whether all the claimed cost benefits were ever really achieved or, if they were, whether they were not outweighed by the problems caused by consequent lack of management information and an inability to understand the very workings of the business itself.

One approach to the problem of shared costs is not to measure them but to negotiate them. The concept of intra-company trading can be a useful one for railway companies in that it avoids the need for tortuous, expensive and often inappropriate cost measurement. It can also have a motivating effect on management, who feel much more in control of their business units, although it clearly has limitations and can be taken too far. Once one has started down this route it leads, of course, to questioning why railways own and operate so many parts of the total travel system themselves anyway. With increasing financial pressures more and more companies will find themselves unable to fund and manage adequately a wide range of diverse activities and this difficulty will increase where right wing governments wish to see less state ownership.

The Role Of The Private Sector

What advantages are there in railways operating and marketing the wide range of products and services which many of them do?

Not cost, as railway cost structures are likely to be higher than those in private industry, and even with intra-company trading there is a real limit to competition within one's own organisation. Probably not financial as it surely must mean spreading scarce capital resources too widely and too thinly. Nor control, as management and product standards are often far better achieved through third party contracts than through railway companies' own systems.

The only real advantage seems to be a marketing one. Railway companies have national networks, high credibility (despite national jokes) and, most importantly, a vast customer base. It is this last property which is probably their single biggest asset and one that it is sensible to exploit with a whole range of individually profitable, ancillary services. But there is no need to own or operate them.

Cross-selling will be the corporate strategy of the late eighties and railway companies are excellently placed to take advantage of this trend. Their market strengths combined with the entrepreneurial skills of private companies, particularly smaller ones, will be able to generate significant profits, but there is not a lot of evidence yet that this is being recognised.

'Sticking to the Knitting' is OK, providing the core activity of the company is profitable. In railways this is often not so and the basic travel products should be viewed more as traffic generators with profit opportunities being sought in the ancillary activities. Governments also

FIG. 2.2. New product development — car servicing for train travellers.

need to recognise this. They will not achieve the financial turn rounds that they are looking for if they too closely constrain their railway companies to just running trains.

An interesting current initiative in this area is British Rail's development of a chain of car servicing and repair centres located in station car parks. Customers think the idea is excellent and it produces substantial net profits. But whilst the development is positioned as a new product, coming from the railway company, it is operated by a private operating company and all the individual units are franchised. This gives BR faster growth and much better quality control whilst at the same time avoiding any potential monopoly problems. There are many other developments which could follow a similar pattern.

Such deliberate moves to work much more closely with private industry are not only sensible commercially but are also important in a much wider strategic way.

It has already been suggested that state ownership is probably not such a good thing for the railway companies of the developed nations. Not because governments interfere in railway affairs, nor because they will not always provide all the funds that railways would like, but principally because, for railway managers, state ownership is both too comfortable, yet at the same time too risky.

The problem with comfort is that managements, no matter how good, get complacent. What is the motivation for that last bit of effort, the bit that actually produces results? Not only does this blunt the railways' effectiveness in the market place, but governments also sense it, and therein lies the risk — the risk of sudden disenchantment which may lead to traumatic results.

The recent decision by the Japanese government to break up and sell off Japanese National Railways resulted from frustration: frustration at mounting deficits, frustration with having no choice but to deal with the railway company generating these deficits, frustration at no apparent alternatives. It provides a timely reminder that such events are 'real possibilities' as JNR's financial, consumer and political position was not much different from other European and North American passenger railway companies. So it is in the interests of the railway companies themselves to press for alternative relationships — and this does not necessarily mean privatisation. We have already talked about joint ventures with the private sector in the development of ancillary products and there are probably similar opportunities for more 'main stream' train travel activities.

But there are also opportunities for developing new ways of managing the national railways themselves. The UK system for awarding franchises for the operation of commercial television services is an interesting model. The regular competition which takes place for these franchises certainly reduces the complacency trap and reduces risk in that the government is not 'stuck' with any one organisation with all the associated tensions and possibility of JNR type actions.

This is not to suggest that this model would be at all appropriate for the management of the whole, or even parts, of a national railway system. It is merely to suggest alternatives, alternatives which railway companies should be exploring and proposing so that the initiative for change remains with them.

Conclusion

The strategic direction described above seems conveniently to ignore the issue as to whether railways can be financially viable or not.

It does not. It argues for a more pragmatic approach which moves the railway companies out of the debate on whether governments should or should not contract for the provision of train services into a position of accepting that they do; and therefore recognising them as customers.

This positioning enables railway companies to re-orientate themselves to a completely commercial, profit objective at the same time as loosening the ties between themselves and governments as shareholders and bankers.

In this way they will realise the enormous market opportunities now open to them.

Jeff Percival is currently National Products and New Ventures Manager at British Rail. He joined British Rail from Heinz. His role in the past few years has been closely related to the changing image of rail travel and the emergence of a more dynamic orientated strategy.

3

The Role Of The Air Carrier

THE GROWTH of air travel has been one of the most noticeable and important social and economic phenomena of the post war period. Starting from a low base point, growth of scheduled international air travel averaged 13% for 25 years. Since the mid 1970s growth has slowed down to average 7% a year, a rate, however, which is still well above growth in income both nationally and individually in the western world. Currently some 190 million passengers are carried by scheduled international airlines and this figure is expected to double before the end of the century.

Simply stated, it is the role of the air carrier to satisfy this demand for transportation. In the real world, unfortunately, nothing is simple and if airlines are to perform their function efficiently then they must overcome a myriad of problems.

It is the purpose of this chapter to outline some of the more important problem areas and to discuss some of the options which air carriers have to choose between if they are to be successful in meeting the changing needs of the marketplace to the satisfaction of both the consumer and of the owners.

Deregulation/Competition

Probably the most prominent issue in civil aviation today is deregulation and its effect on the structure of the air transport industry.

The post war air transport industry grew up in a strictly controlled environment, justified in part by the needs of an infant industry and by a concern to establish common standards worldwide in technical, operational and commercial areas. Without governmental intervention and cooperation between airlines, the development of air travel would have been less orderly than has been the case.

In the United States, however, during the seventies, it began to be felt that the industry had outgrown the need for external control and that both the industry and its customers would benefit if regulation were to be withdrawn. Consequently, in 1978 the US government introduced legislation deregulating routes within the USA and in 1979 brought in an act concerning competition on international routes. Faced with a choice between a partial or gradual withdrawal of control and a complete overnight change, the US authorities opted for the latter course. Seven years later the effects of the changeover are still being studied and it is felt that the entire process has not yet been completed.

The changes deregulation made in the States were by no means entirely what had been anticipated. There have been benefits to the customer in areas of choice of airline and lower prices but there has been a price to pay as routes have disappeared and airlines have become bankrupted. The present concern is whether or not the largest and most successful airlines may not in the next few years become so dominant that they will be able to exercise monopolistic powers over their markets at the expense of the passenger. There is also concern about the long term financial stability of the industry; and a solution here is difficult to see unless either some companies leave the business or there are mergers between airlines; in other words fewer airlines. Were this to happen, then the purpose of deregulation, i.e. to pass the benefits of competition (lower prices, greater choice) on to the customer, would to a large extent be defeated.

The rest of the world of aviation, especially the Europeans, are watching the unfolding scene in the States with great interest in order to learn from the experience there and decide whether the lessons learned there would apply in other markets. In Europe there are voices calling for as complete a deregulation as possible, given the greater complexity in the structure of the air market there compared to the USA. At the same time other voices feel that progress should be evolutionary and that some control of schedules, prices, routes, licences etc., should remain with governments or their agencies. The main uncertainty is the speed at which change is introduced. Each month sees a further erosion of the bastions of regulation in Europe and it is not difficult to see many major markets becoming more fully competitive within two or three years.

Elsewhere in the world more competition and deregulation is proceeding, led by the South-East Asian airlines; and it is to be expected that the whole of the Pacific Basin area (which is forecast to have the greatest growth during the rest of the century) will see intense competition and the growth of sixth freedom carriage focusing on the major hubs of the region.

Deregulation is like Pandora's box — once the process has started there is no turning back. The international air travel market is poised to undergo a fundamental change as striking as anything in its history. To survive and prosper, airlines will have to learn the art of studying the consumer and meeting his changing needs swiftly and at minimum cost.

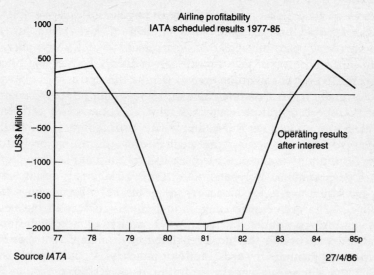

FIG. 3.1. Airline profitability: IATA scheduled results 1977-85.

Funding/Profitability

Another major issue facing air transport operators is how to find the capital necessary for the replacement of their existing fleet and, moreover, to expand that fleet to meet growing demand.

The facts are bleak; for the last 20 years the cost of new aircraft has been increasing in real terms. This cost increase is at a greater rate than the saving from improvements in efficiency that new designs can give. Over this same period airline revenues have been squeezed hard and yield has declined in real terms. The result of these pressures is that in 1984/5, a boom year in traffic demand, IATA airlines made a profit collectively that was well short of what is necessary in the long term to generate sufficient funds to improve the debt equity ratio to more acceptable levels and to ensure the replacement of ageing fleets with more efficient aircraft. If the financial target cannot be met in the boom periods then the outlook in the longer term is gloomy indeed.

What possibilities exist for an improvement? Could aircraft become cheaper? Can airlines become more efficient and hence more profitable? Is there any other alternative?

The likelihood of cheaper aircraft is not dependent on strictly commercial considerations.

Profits from a particular model depend on sales running into several hundred within a relatively short time of the inception of a development programme. Few models in the past have succeeded in reaching these targets. However, competition between European and American designs will influence the terms offered to airlines. Additionally, governments, conscious of wider issues such as balance of payments, level of employment and the need to encourage the development of high technology, may intervene to influence the choice of design and the cost to the purchaser.

Part of the problem of high aircraft cost is due to the fact that prices are quoted in US dollars and at the time of writing this currency is over-valued by 20% or so. If this situation changes, there would be some benefit.

Air transport operators can, and must, become more efficient but whether that improvement will lead to greater profitability is doubtful since competitive pressures are forcing yield downwards. A major feature of airline profitability in the past has been its cyclical nature, coinciding with the 4/5 year economic cycle, and the extreme variability in results between peak and trough years. The long run average has never been enough to meet the financial target of generating enough funds to stay in business. Of course, in the past airlines were not always required to meet such standards of performance due to the more regulated environment that existed and governmental attitudes towards an infant industry. A considerable amount of ingenuity will be necessary in the future, as ownership of airlines passes away from governments or as governments set more stringent standards for state owned operators.

One development that may help with this problem is through the leasing of aircraft rather than outright purchase. Financial leases for the whole operating life of an aircraft offer opportunities of avoiding the need to raise capital if conditions should be unfavourable and also the possibility of benefiting from the tax allowances to lessors which airlines, with their low profits, are not positioned to take advantage of.

Operating leases which cover shorter-term periods, typically of one to three years, offer airlines the chance to respond to unexpected changes in demand more rapidly than through purchase. This ability may be crucial in the more competitive arena of the future in enabling airlines to maximise revenue, protect their market shares and optimise profits.

Privatisation/Ownership

Alongside the debate over the issue of deregulation is a related issue of ownership of airlines. Outside the USA, a vast number of international airlines started life as government-owned. This was natural in the early post-war days, since the regulated environment that existed at that time was not conducive to entrants to the industry that were not agents of a nation's air transport policy. Additionally, the amount of capital required to start an airline was not readily available. Today, the situation is one of change. Governments still, by and large, own the major international scheduled companies but there is a trend in many countries for governmental involvement to lessen. The impetus for this development comes from a change in perception of the nature of the air transport business following the introduction of deregulation in the United States and its spread across the Atlantic into other international air markets.

Air transport is increasingly being viewed as being just another industry and subject to the same rules of supply and demand, and to the same financial yardsticks of performance as apply to other industries. In such circumstances arguments for lessening governmental control become stronger. The management of airlines resent government interference in major commercial decisions, for example aircraft purchase, and which routes to operate, since governments often have different objectives: to protect an embryo aircraft manufacturing industry, to avoid balance of payment difficulties, to develop the tourist industry and so on. While these objectives are desirable enough in themselves, they are not relevant to the efficient operation of an air transport business and may compromise efficiency.

Governments have other reasons for wishing to distance themselves. The governmental balance sheet can benefit from the sale of assets which release funds for use elsewhere in the economy. They can avoid association with a business that has rarely in the past been financially successful; finally there are many politicians who argue that running businesses is not the affair of the government.

How far will this trend go?

Essentially the decision is a political one, determined by the degree of commitment to policies of public ownership vis-a-vis private, favoured by governments of left or right wing persuasion. The issue is also influenced by national policies regarding the development of the air transport industry and the absolute size and importance of that industry relative to the rest of the economy.

Another determinant may be the performance of the airline: the more successful it is, the more shares will be worth and the easier it will be to sell them to private interests. But these factors will only come into account if a government decides that it should play a less influential role.

It is probable that most governments will remain majority shareholders, retaining control of what is often regarded as a vital part of a country's economic infrastructure. The more purist approach of a complete sale, as in the case of British Airways, may be unique for some time, until the benefits predicted by its management from their commercial freedom are realised.

Distribution

One of the most crucial areas of airline activity is the distribution process. In this arena battles for marketplace dominance will occur as the system develops the ability to use the latest electronic technology and to structure itself for efficiency and customer service. The relationship between the airlines and the travel agents will come under strain as they both seek to influence customer choice and gain a dominant hold.

The airlines have three driving forces: firstly, the need to reduce, as far as possible, the cost of making sales; secondly, to avoid a situation where they become dominated by the retailers, lose their identity and become mere providers of seating capacity; thirdly, to stop being subject to the whims of a distribution system they have to share — the airline which has best control of its distribution system will be the most successful. The retailers' main problem is to avoid being cut out altogether from the selling process between passengers and airline, but they too have to offer an increasingly comprehensive service at the lowest possible cost.

For the airlines the solution to lower distribution costs lies in automation and more direct links, both developments which hit at the role of the retailer. Avoiding domination by large multiple retailers calls for the promotion of a strongly branded image sold direct to the public where possible.

The retailer, however, must seek economies of scale and also concentrate on marketing products which call for the unique expertise and experience they possess.

Today many airlines in the States and elsewhere have developed advanced reservation systems on computers, which simplify the task of the travel agent in making bookings on their flights. Taking this a step further, the most successful and largest of these systems have been developed to provide a service for several subscribing carriers, but there are doubts raised about their neutrality in use. Assuming these fears are allayed, then the spread of this facility worldwide is merely a matter of time. There is a great deal of money to be made by those airlines whose systems become most widely adopted, not only in gaining more customers, but also from user charges to other subscribers.

There are, however, many other developments which will change the face of marketing air travel. The most obvious are the possibilities for consumers to link up to the airlines reservation system through their television sets. They will be able to scan timetables, make bookings and pay for them through the same medium without leaving their armchairs. The brochure will be replaced by a video film, showing more vividly the choice of destination and accommodation available. It will also be possible to use home computers in a similar way, to access travel information. Another development, at present in its infancy, but with considerable potential for the future, is the personal travel centre, a machine set up in public places — airports, department stores, etc., which can be interrogated for travel information and can also, in conjunction with credit cards, issue tickets. The attraction for the consumer is obvious, since information will be available when he wants it — no worrying about shop hours. The advantage for the airline is also great: lower sales costs because of fewer sales and reservations staff, less reliance on travel agents.

There is another side to the coin, however, since these electronic devices are less well suited to journeys of a more complicated nature. The public is generally (and naturally) rather apprehensive of relying on machines when the task is not simple and the convolutions of international air tariffs and routings sometimes dismay even the professionals, whose job it is daily to find the quickest and cheapest itinerary for their clients.

Another market that will resist the electronic invasion is the holiday-maker who wishes to choose a new destination, or a holiday with non-standard features. Doubtless he will be able to browse through pages on a TV programme just as he can look through a brochure, but many people will prefer a situation where they can discuss alternatives with someone who has first-hand experience of the products on offer. There is undoubtedly a role here for specialist retailers, but to ensure their success they will have to maintain and improve the quality of their service because it is that aspect which is unique.

A View Of The Future

If the future demand for air travel is to be satisfied, then airline operators must form a view of the most important likely developments so that they can develop strategies to deal successfully with the sometimes conflicting needs of the market and consumer on the one hand and of the company on the other.

What, then, can be reliably said about the future? Firstly, it is highly probable that the number of air journeys made will increase substantially. A consensus of forecasts from aircraft manufacturers and airlines points to a market size, before the end of the century, roughly double that of today. Secondly, it is highly likely that the industry will be less regulated, leading to more intense competition between airlines. Thirdly, the consumer will become even more demanding both as a consequence of competition giving a greater choice and also arising from greater familiarity as the experience of air travel becomes steadily more widespread. Fourthly, regardless of the outcome of possible changes in ownership from the public to the private sector, all airlines are going to be increasingly required to produce an adequate return on capital invested. Lastly, it is unlikely, in pursuit of the goal of better profits, that improved cost effectiveness from advances in aircraft technology or from higher unit revenues will offset the reductions in yield obtainable in a more competitive marketplace to any great extent.

All these factors present a sobering outlook for airline operators and they will need all their resources to overcome the challenges ahead.

Let us look at what can or should be done within the airline.

Firstly, there will have to be very tight cost controls if profitability targets

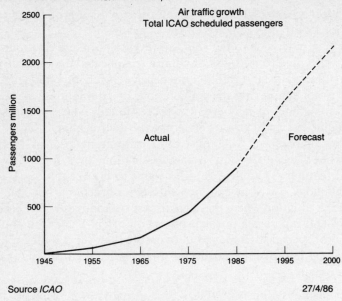

FIG. 3.2. Air traffic growth: total ICAO scheduled passengers.

are to be met. Low costs will be an essential part of an airline's ability to meet and counter threats from competitors. The major components of cost for an airline are:

a) the cost of acquiring and maintaining a suitable fleet of aircraft
b) fuel costs
c) the wage bill.

Taking first the cost of aircraft, we have already noted that this has tended to drift upwards in real terms and new aircraft types have, in the past, cost more compared to older types, though it is possible to offset this through lower operating costs resulting from technological advance. In these circumstances airlines are choosing to operate their existing aircraft for longer. For some airlines there are opportunities for increasing the utilisation of their aircraft through more efficient scheduling but many of the major operators have already practically exhausted possibilities in this area: there are limits to the number of slots at major airports and the availability of commercial timings. Such companies can, however, ensure that those flights which are operated are analysed rigorously to ensure that they provide the optimal overall result for the airline. (Not an easy task in a dynamic marketplace.)

Fuel costs do not offer much opportunity for cost control for airline management since the price of fuel is determined externally. It is vital to ensure that the most efficient aircraft are used and that advantage is taken whenever possible of buying fuel in the cheapest markets. This in itself can be a very complicated process for a large airline, as prices vary quite considerably at airports throughout the world and this affects the uplift of fuel over and above the operational need.

Improving manpower productivity offers some opportunities for airlines to tackle in seeking cost reductions. This has certainly been the experience in the United States in the post-deregulation conditions. Some major carriers there have negotiated tough deals with their unions. Two-tier wage systems have been introduced whereby new staff are paid at lower rates than existing employees. Such practices have been made possible in the States because many categories of airline employees have been amongst the highest paid in the country and thus it was possible to attract new staff even at the lower rates. The appearance of low cost airlines such as People Express have intensified the spread of this trend. People Express have also pioneered the concept of job flexibility in which many employees perform more than one basic function. Whether such practices will continue now remains to be seen, but the message of the need to increase labour productivity cannot be ignored.

Controlling costs is one part of the equation for success for the airline. Revenue maximisation is another. If this goal is to be achieved, then the airline has to make the most of the market opportunities which exist. In the future this task will be more difficult than ever before with more aggressive competition and more discerning customers. Airlines will have to get closer to their customers to understand their needs and even anticipate them if possible. When the customers' wants and preferences are understood, then the airline must act swiftly to provide the services required. The changes required may involve intangibles like more friendly service from cabin crew, check-in and reservations staff; or they may concern improvements to the schedule, better connections, more comfortable seating and higher standards of catering, faster reservations service, etc. Enhancing all these services costs money but there is a constant pressure to provide them at a lower price or at least one which offers better value for money. Finally, the successful airline will be the one that not only understands the customer best and anticipates his needs correctly but also chooses to be in the market that best suits the characteristics of that particular company. Some companies may succeed in offering a worldwide network of services to a wide range of market segments. Others may concentrate on one particular area of the market either geographically or in terms of specific market segment. Whichever the path chosen, the fundamental principle will remain that the markets served must be profitable.

Alongside the need for identifying profitable market opportunities and customer requirements is the necessity of providing the service promised at the highest possible standard, consistently: quality control, in other words. The problem presented has two conflicting aspects: firstly, the need to keep up with the market leaders in order not to lose market share: secondly, to do so as quickly and cheaply as possible, so that profits do not suffer. In seeking this goal it may not pay to be an innovator. It may be a better strategy to copy successful changes, but to do so swiftly.

The message for airline management is quite clear: the successful airline in the future controls its costs and reacts more quickly and more sensitively to the market than its competitors, for if it fails it will quickly become unprofitable — a situation which may be much less acceptable than in the past.

The key aspect of the future which keeps returning is the speed of change and the consequent need for speed of reaction. The underlying assumption is that air markets will become less regulated, so that it will be easier for existing airlines to compete on routes previously not available and it will also be easier for new airlines to start operations hoping to attract business away from existing airlines and also to serve markets not served at present. These developments will probably bring imbalances between capacity and demand, and these, together with more airlines competing, will force prices down further and faster than has been the trend in the past. The fall in airline yields in real terms, over the past decades, has been mainly as a consequence of productivity improvements as aircraft have become more efficient. Cost savings of this type will still occur, but they are unlikely to offset completely the downward pressure on yield stemming from increased competition.

A further recourse for airlines, apart from savings in capital expenditure and manpower, will be to optimise the occupation of the seats on sale by differential pricing to a wider variety of market segments and by the adoption of stringent controls matching the capacity offered to the expected demand, segment by segment. Success in the pursuit of these policies will come not only by accurately predicting the relative size of each price segment served but by carefully balancing the relative size of each segment to ensure the maximum revenue is earned by each flight. The main difficulty in achieving an optimum balance for yield is in the accurate prediction of demand in each price bracket. The problem is compounded by the fact that the highest yielding categories — the first class passengers and the businessman — usually book last and therefore it is not easy to avoid a situation where all the seats in an aircraft are sold to low-yield holiday-makers before the more profitable customers have decided which flight they require. This problem will need the use of more sophisticated computerised controls governing the number of seats available in each price category during the months and weeks before travel. The booking characteristics of flights vary considerably, but small improvements in accuracy of matching supply with demand will make a crucial contribution to the success or otherwise of airlines.

What of the customers of the future? How different will they be from today's users of air transport? What demands will they be making tomorrow? Can their expectations be met?

Traditionally, the air travel market has always been split between two major groups: the business traveller and the leisure market. As noted earlier, general predictions of growth over the next 10—15 years have been in the range of 5%—7% per year leading to a doubling in size of the total market worldwide over that time. Obviously there will be considerable differences in growth rate in various parts of the world, depending upon such variables as growth in GNP and per capita personal disposable income, market maturity, current levels of wealth, etc. However, throughout the western world it is probable that growth in business travel will be exceeded by growth in the leisure sector. Increased personal income levels together with increased amounts of leisure time will drive the growth of the leisure market while sociological trends in the developed countries also predict smaller family units with a probably higher level of disposable income as a common phenomenon. Another probable trend will be a turning away from package holidays towards more individual products as people become more familiar with foreign travel and travel agents widen the combination of choice available. This trend will be encouraged by the fact that in many countries the age group which is most increasing in size is the 35—45 year old as the growth segment of the past, the 20s—30s, mature.

Although the business traveller is not expected to provide spectacular growth his preferences will not be ignored, because of his ability to pay. One development which may have an important influence on business travel is the facility to hold tele-conferences. Opinions differ widely regarding the impact this may have on business travel. Some think that many business journeys would be rendered unnecessary by the widespread adoption of this means of communication. Others believe that the majority of business journeys fall into categories which will be relatively undisturbed, for example, the need to make personal contact, which electronic devices cannot replace, the element of perk/status represented by some business trips, the ability to contact several customers or suppliers and to inspect goods or services physically.

The business traveller will continue to be discerning and this characteristic will be enhanced by increased competition. Airlines may seek ways of retaining the loyalty of the business customers through devices such as the loyalty scheme seen in the US or a variety of ancillary services. Unfortunately these practices lead to lower yields, which means costs have to be cut, leading to lower service standards: a roundabout of uncertainty. Carriers will have to decide whether they can successfully provide high cost products to all major segments or whether they must concentrate on one market niche, and provide the product that that niche wants.

Nobody in the airline industry expects the future to be easy. The large airlines have certain advantages, particularly in being able to offer a range of services to suit most markets. The smaller airlines can adapt more easily and rapidly and match the needs of particular markets more closely; but there is no guarantee of success for anyone. The most elusive and desirable attribute is vision, which enables any company to position itself to exploit the opportunities as they arise, or, better still, anticipate those opportunities. Few airlines will be able to regard particular markets as their own property in the future. Equally they may seek business in markets which have never been available before. Mergers may occur between airlines operating in different regions of the world; sixth freedom traffic will become more important to many carriers as they seek to exploit the growth routes/areas. There will be no one formula for success beyond quick reactions and a steady nerve. There is, equally, no doubt that the next few years will be very interesting for all those trying to grapple with these forces and come out at the end running a successful business.

Alan Wheeler is currently concentrating on market planning and development for British Airways. He has been with BA for many years and has closely observed the fluctuating and changing fortunes of the world's airlines. He is very conscious of the need for strategic focus and he is, as a result of his years of experience, playing a crucial role in the future development of his company.

4

The Travel Agent —
Rise Or Fall?

A Review Of The Travel Agent's Role And Future

In any discussion of the travel and tourist industry, the travel agent is often an afterthought: a necessary, but not very influential, member of the manufacturing and distribution chain, and certainly the least mature. It is seen as the last of the litter, a sector condemned to an early death. Others see it as the sector having the most to prove. The 1990s will provide the answer: but those already writing travel agents off must remember that they have the potential to become equal partners, if not leaders, in the business.

Observers of the tourist trade at the beginning of the 1980s might have been tempted to see travel agents as a weak, indeterminate mass. There was little difference between them and, as companies or as a sector, they tended singularly to fail to present a coherent image either to their customers or their subscribers. A few travel agents had international networks; fewer still had managed to exploit them. There was little attempt to recognise the different needs of different customers and, with a few notable exceptions, business travellers and leisure travellers tended to be treated as one and the same. Few countries saw any multiple travel agents with more than 10% of the total market. Principals still tended to treat multiple travel agents as a group of individual, independent outlets, servicing only a selection of branches; and felt no obligation or irresistible pressure to deal with any multiple travel agent. The situation in 1980 reflected the exceptional immaturity of the travel agency sector.

Things may have changed since 1980, but even by the beginning of 1986, the sector had only just entered its adolescence. A current comparison of the sector with other retail or corporate service sectors in the economy soon makes it clear that there is much to be done. The sector is still dominated by small businesses, some highly effective and profitable, but the vast majority relatively unproductive and lacking in innovation; there is still some way to go before the major multiples will have anything like the dominance that multiple retailers have in other sectors. For instance, in 1984 the largest UK holiday travel agent had only an 8.5% market share. Indeed, the top three multiple agents had only 18% market share between them. But there were clear signs of change, which continued throughout 1985 and into 1986. A flurry of takeovers in the UK saw, over these years, the top three agents moving from having 500 outlets to over 800. Mergers and takeovers abounded elsewhere — indeed, few of the major developed countries failed to witness such a change. Real signs were evident of the growth of international travel agency chains and groupings, catering to the needs of the business traveller worldwide and beginning to use purchasing power, coupled with new communication technology, to produce a range of products and services which showed real differences.

TABLE 1 Association Of British Travel Agents

	1977	1978	1979	1980	1981	1982	1983	1984	1985
No. of Agencies	3814	3989	4201	4398	4781	5055	5299	5720	6003

Source: ABTA; sum of number of companies in Retail Agents Class and number of branches. ABTA

Number of Branches per Retail Member	2.19	2.12	2.22	2.26	2.28	2.29	2.22	2.26	2.27

Source: ABTA

Yet despite this, the independent travel agent still had the substantial share of the business world-wide. It is this historic, if increasingly irrelevant, structure of the sector which still pervades the relationship between supplier and agent. The legal dependency of principal and agent is often reflected in an attempt to retain an equivalent psychological dependency. As a result, the attitude of some suppliers/principals to travel agents can tend towards the indulgent arrogance typical of the individually powerful towards the individually weak. Suppliers' commercial negotiations are complemented by the investment of substantial funds into maintaining goodwill and dependence through entertainment and incentives. It is a relationship which many agents are happy to accept and one indeed, which is suitable to their business. However, it is one that disguises the changing balance of power between the principal and the agent as it moves rapidly to that of supplier and retailer. It has been increasingly important for suppliers to recognise the difference between the various parts of their distribution network, and alter the nature and style of their commercial relationship accordingly. The first half of the 1980s has seen a growing acceptance of this change.

One Business Or Many?

One of the driving forces behind the change in the role and attitude of travel agents has been the growing sophistication and increasing demands of the customer. This change has influenced the marketing strategies of principals; new aircraft configurations, segmentation of tour operator products and new hotel facilities. The agent has not been immune either. The time when a travel agent could simply sell an air ticket, catering for any type of customer, through one outlet is almost over. The seats may be on the same flight and to the same destination, but individual customers' demands may be radically different. The business traveller needs one type of service, the family holidaymaker another: both expect a different service and product from the younger bargain hunter. Segmentation has been a centrepiece of developments throughout all retailing in the 1980s, and travel is no exception. A single outlet or image can no longer appeal across the total range of potential customers. The travel agency sector is splitting into different businesses, at one level into business travel, group travel, incentive travel: but beyond that into outlets reflecting different lifestyles and cultures.

Travellers will argue that these differences have been around for a long time; however, it is only in the 1980s that, facing increased competition for a limited customer base coupled with growing customer sophistication, the travel agency sector has recognised and exploited them. For instance, 10 years ago it was normal to conduct a strong business travel operation within the same premises and under the same management as a leisure travel business; now few multiple agencies would attempt this. Instead, business travel has been split out of the high street retail shops into purpose-made office units equipped with specialised staff and technology. In many cases, this has been accompanied by much more specific marketing activities with the development of separate logos, sales forces and advertising strategy.

Customer demand has not only meant the need for different services for different customers, but also for different management styles. The travel agency sector consists very definitely of a mix of businesses where the differences between each business are rapidly becoming more important than the similarities.

The Business Traveller

Who is this mythical person — the business traveller? For the traveller, him or herself, the needs of the business traveller may be self evident. But for the travel agent there is rarely any one such coherent body as the business traveller and, even if there is, he or she only represents half the travel agents' equation in meeting the needs of this sector of the business.

The truth is that the concept of the business traveller is as segmented, if not more segmented, than that of the holidaymaker. From one perspective there are three types of business travellers;

— the 'do it yourself' business traveller
— 'do as allowed' business traveller
— 'do as told' business traveller

Which category any business traveller falls into depends on a variety of factors, the predominant one being the type of company or organisation to which he or she belongs. But also of importance is the culture of the organisation and the position the business traveller holds.

A 'do it yourself' business traveller is one who makes bookings with airlines, hotels and even travel agents either directly or through his or her secretary. This could typically be either the individual small businessman or an executive of a major corporation. While there is a growing trend for large companies to control their travel budget, a high proportion of companies, both in Europe and the USA, exert no structure on their employees' travel.

The 'do as allowed' and the 'do as told' business travellers reflect different levels of control within corporations; some set regulations or allowances within which business travellers make their own arrangements; others centralise travel through a travel department which makes the arrangements for executives. Each type of business travel structure demands a different type of approach by the travel agent, and a successful business travel agent has to be able to bridge the gap, within the same servicing outlet, between those requiring individual service and those being serviced through central corporate travel departments.

But however the account is operated, the ultimate needs of the business traveller are not that dissimilar and centre on reliability, efficiency, ability to deal with problems and an understanding of his personal needs. It is almost invariably failure in these areas of service that loses travel agents accounts.

But while the needs of the business traveller may well seem relatively clear cut to the traveller himself, for the travel agent there is another dimension to business travel; the corporate accounts' financial director or controller. While an account may be lost on service, it is increasingly being won on price and cost control. The travel agent is faced with the standard retailing dilemma of striking the balance between price and quality. The problem is that, as is not the case with individual travel, these two conflicting dimensions belong to two different parts of the corporate structure. It is common within corporations that the decision-maker is not a regular traveller. Increasingly the decision has been made by somebody who is concerned with financial control and is not personally aware of the needs of the business traveller and the hidden cost implications of poor service.

There is some evidence that this myopia is changing and there is a growing awareness among corporations that to insist upon the cheapest flight or hotel may backfire, affecting badly, as it does, the performance of an executive at his or her destination. More emphasis is being paid by both corporate customer and travel agent alike on the quality and the width of the service offered.

Market Positioning

Roger Hymas in Chapter 7 illustrates how business travel can become part of wider financial control and management service. Business travel agents face fundamental strategic decisions about their future direction as the industry and the customer becomes more mature and the top multiples take an ever-increasing share of the market. As the market moves away from price, agents have to develop unique selling propositions and positioning across the following dimensions:

domestic — international
individual service — highly automated centres
travel expertise — business consultancy/servicing
price — value added services

The major business travel agents are settling into their respective but different positions on this four-dimensional matrix. They still tend, however, to assume that they will be able to appeal to a wide range of business travellers. This will not work. Different clients will want different forms of distribution and service. Success for the business travel agent will largely depend on picking the right market sector and tailoring the product to meet that sector's needs and then building up a range of services and identities to tackle the individual differences within that sector as a whole. The travel agent may be expert in dealing with large multinational corporations but it still has to differentiate between the needs of the Chairman and the frequent flyer.

Direct Sell; The Principals' Dilemma

There is an underlying assumption in this analysis that the business travel agent will continue to have a major role to play until the end of the century. There are many who would wish to challenge this assumption. As the multiple travel agents get larger, so some principals, in particular airlines, are continually searching for ways of bypassing them. These methods range from operating their own shops and outlets to trying to develop electronic means which will allow direct booking either from a travel department of a corporation or by the business traveller himself. Indeed, there has been success in this field in the USA, where there is a deregulated airline market. The majority of travel is domestic, and there are highly effectively marketed national hotel chains. In this environment no one business travel agent has obtained any real dominance.

There are many barriers to such a scenario developing in Europe or elsewhere in the world — the conditions of the market are substantially different. The only real message an airline has to its business customers in support of direct marketing is price (cutting out the agents' commission may theoretically allow it to discount its fares). But price is becoming less dominant as a feature in the market-place. The battleground has moved towards choice, expertise and value-added services. In these cases the travel agent has an advantage, not least because, within the regulated market, most major travel agents have negotiated special fares which are not available through an airline's servicing unit. On top of that, travel agents are supporting corporate accounts with management information, free additional services and, in many cases, staff. Unless corporate accounts have very structured travel patterns a single airline booking operation is unlikely to be attractive.

In looking towards direct sell methods, the suppliers have a dilemma. The greatest demand for direct sell comes in sectors where convenience is the major decision-making variable and brand identity is less relevant. The greater difference and distinction there is between products, the more the customer will look to a retailer to help him or her through the maze of features and benefits. The one thing the suppliers in the travel industry are most fearful of is simply becoming a commodity with no distinction between their product and others. Airlines fear decisions being made simply on when they fly and not on the quality of their service. Hoteliers spend vast amounts of money extolling their differences.

The future of business travel agents may lie in the hands of the suppliers — but suppliers will not successfully lose the cost of dealing with agents without also risking losing their differential and brand identity.

Holiday/Vacational Travel — Agent Or Retailer?

Whereas there is evidence of growing internationalism within the business travel market, the same cannot be said in the vacational field. The nature of vacational travel varies dramatically from country to country, with the prevalence of overseas package holidays in the North European countries to the dominance of the directly marketed and booked domestic industry in the USA.

Furthermore, the shape of travel retailing is severely influenced by the general state and style of retailing in those countries. Therefore in the UK, for instance, travel retailing takes its place in competition for disposable income primarily on the high street of the cities and towns. The state of retailing there is distinctly different from that in, for example, New Zealand or Spain. The nature and size of the vacational travel retailing business will be a function of the country's vacational travel and shopping habits. The successful travel retailer will be the one that finds the right products, image and format for its particular market's vacational travel shopping habits.

This chapter tends to concentrate on the holiday travel retailer in the UK in the hope and expectation that the reader will translate and interpret the validity of the statements to their own environment.

The development of travel retailing over the past decade in the UK has followed a trend set by other sectors of the retailing industry in the 1960s and 1970s. There have been a number of collapses or takeovers among the small and medium sized chains, leaving national multiples and strong regional or local independents dominating the industry. This has happened at a time when the number of agents has actually increased. As there is still a relatively low cost of entry (the combination of these trends can be seen in Table 1 where the rapid growth in ABTA outlets has only produced a marginal shift in the number of outlets per member). Until the role of the travel agent really turns into one of a retailer, these two trends are likely to continue, with the increasing size of the multiples being matched by an increasing number of agents. If and when the large multiples have the purchasing power to buy stock and also have the legal right to alter price, then the industry will enter the next stage of its rationalisation. Both these possibilities are likely to happen in the 1980s so that, by 1990, it can be expected that the industry will again be more concentrated.

In deciding strategy and market positioning any retailer has a number of key decision variables. Having determined the target customer profile the retailer can vary:

— shop location
— shop design
— product range
— price
— staff and service levels

The resultant mix should generate a clear image and position in the market-place which can be communicated to the customer through advertising and promotional activities. Travel agents are no exception: the same strategic decisions face their management. Those that have both tackled them and developed a coherent approach to their retail business are still few and far between.

Shop Location

In a period where the travel agent had little influence on price and there was not a great distinction between different travel agents' product range, then shop location became vital. It was important enough in the 1970s but in the early 1980s, with a higher proportion of travel arrangements/holidays being

TTI - E

made at short notice or on an impulse basis, then location became increasingly critical.

Most research shows that a large proportion of holidaymakers have traditionally made their initial choice of travel agent on the basis of convenience, just as they do with most other service retailers. They have gone to the nearest travel agent which looks reasonable and treats them satisfactorily. Only if they have had problems there, or if they are looking for a more complicated or unusual product or service, will they make the effort to find a better known professional operation. So whereas they might well be exceptionally discriminating in their choice of travel agency for their round-the-world 'once in a lifetime' trip, customers will be far less discriminating initially for the yearly package holiday in Spain.

Most travel agents are located in secondary retail sites in the UK. Only Thomas Cook, among the large chains in the UK, has had a consistent policy to look for prime sites. Most travel companies have looked for growth through acquisition of other agents, therefore perpetuating their positioning in secondary locations. Indeed the nature of the travel industry does allow a secondary location strategy — as evidenced by the fact that Thomas Cook has launched a second chain, Frames, to take advantage of this secondary location market.

As a general rule, retailers will generate sales volume in proportion to passing pedestrian flow. However, because they hold no stock, it is possible for poorly located travel agents to take the goods to the customer, either through the creation of special products advertised in the local press, or by active promotions in major venues in the town. Many good independents have built up a very strong loyal customer base by these and other methods. With a once a year purchase, which is psychologically so important, personal service and initiative can overcome location problems.

However, good location is important in developing a national image; until 1985 only Thomas Cook had consistently developed an image through national television and press advertising. Attempts by other multiple travel agents to advertise nationally had been undermined by the inconvenience of their locations, their customers' ignorance of their existence, and their inability as yet to find a sufficiently strong differential to persuade a substantial number of new customers to overcome these factors. 1985 saw a change as Thomas Cook's exclusive position in this regard was challenged by Lunn Poly, once the retail subsidiary of Thomson Travel. 1986 has seen Pickfords Travel taking a more prominent profile in this medium. With a newly created national chain, Lunn Poly gained a substantial market share by heavy national advertising and a successful pseudo-discount promotion — illustrating how in the travel industry location problems can be overcome at a national, as well as local, level by creating price differentials. (Lunn Polly is now owned by Pickfords.)

But price can quickly be matched in a market share fight — location cannot. In a short term battle for growth, the well-located chain will always have the edge. While there may be no hard and fast rules as to the relationship of shop location and profitability, one of the major criticisms that can be aimed at most multiple travel agents in the UK is the inconsistency of their policy and the confusion which that causes themselves and their customers.

The decision whether to go to a prime location is not totally under control of travel agency management. Many planners and shop centre developers still classify travel agents as Grade 2 retailers in the UK, i.e. alongside banks, building societies etc. They regard them as failing to generate additional passenger flow but rather simply servicing existing business. Again, only Thomas Cook has managed to have itself accepted as a Grade 1 retailer throughout most of the country, a change which has largely stemmed from its approach to shop design. Good locations require investment in time, people and design, not just money.

Shop Design

The general standard of shop layout and design in UK travel agencies has been very poor, reflecting the tendency to view them as offices not shops. It is an area of considerable difference and not one where the multiples have been significantly better than independents. Most multiples now have clean and uncluttered branches but there have been few attempts to develop a style or design image. Given their secondary locations and the fact that they are not therefore having to compete for share of voice with the mainstream retailers, this is perhaps not surprising. The design concepts of the more successful multiples reflect their positioning in the market-place; Thomas Cook, with an aggressive, fashion-based design aimed at attracting customers in prime high street locations, and companies such as Pickfords and Lunn Poly who have developed effective but functional design concepts which are suitable for their good secondary locations and are easy to introduce into other travel agencies they acquire as part of their expansion programmes. (Figure 4.1 shows changes in shop design at Thomas Cook between 1973 and 1985.)

Design, of course, is now recognised as a fundamental key to success in retailing. UK high streets are now showpieces of rapidly changing design concepts to attract different market sectors; there is no doubt that travel agents, in coming to terms with their role as retailers rather than agents, will also have to come to terms with the requirements of shop design. With other service sectors such as post offices, building societies and banks investing substantial money in shop design, customers' expectations are increasing. Poor design, scruffy branches and untidy display will reduce sales. As with other retail market segments, the functional all-purpose all-customer designs will also begin to lose their appeal. Customers expect in branches design characteristics which appeal to them and their, needs and will be attracted far more to retailers who gear themselves to those needs than those who try to provide an environment that appeals as much to an 18 as to an 80 year old.

There is no doubt that the area of shop design and layout is one with the greatest potential for revolutionary change. While some retailers have upgraded their style of operation substantially, few, if any, have succeeded with merchandising: the best way to display and distribute their product range. The problems in this area are a consequence of the fact that travel agents do not have a physical product to display. While they may, like fashion retailers, be selling dreams, they do not have the dreams in the shop to be taken away or tried on. Indeed, their only concrete product is a holiday brochure. There have been various attempts to overcome this by using media such as video, but so far without real success. Window displays, in particular, generally compare very poorly with other retailers.

Despite, and perhaps because of, these problems, design has become an area where the travel retailer can differentiate his shop from his competitors', providing a strong conscious and subconscious message to the potential customer about the style and image of the products and services being offered. The combination of shop location and shop design has been shown to make a significant difference to sales volume, reinforcing again the view that the agent is more alike than different from other high street retailers.

But well-designed and located shops are not just important for the individual agent, but to the travel agency industry as a whole. Holidays are vying with other consumer durables for the limited disposable income available. Well-located and designed travel shops are therefore fundamental to the continuing growth in the holiday market, bringing the product to the forefront of the customer's attention. Furthermore, if the travel agency industry does not take this highly aggressive role as retailers, then it will increasingly undermine the reason for its continued existence. The travel agency sector cannot afford to continue to have an image of being reactive order-takers, responding to a business generated by the activities of the principals. If they do, the time will come when the principals will find a cheaper and more controllable distribution mechanism.

Product

One of the most significant changes that has taken place in the strategy of travel agents over the past 10 years, has been the major reassessment of their product range policy. It is a further example of the move away from being an agent and into being a retailer.

The products a travel agent sells are partly determined by licences and partly by marketing position. Only a relatively small proportion (around

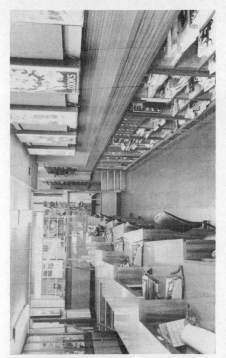

Fig 4.1. Design concepts should reflect the desired market position: The development of design in branches.

25%) of UK travel outlets have an IATA licence, enabling them to ticket airline sales. This is in great contrast to other parts of the world where airline sales are the major component of a travel agent's business. In the UK the majority of travel agents' prime product is package holidays and a large proportion of them continue the tradition of selling any product or brand a customer requests, provided the tour operator belongs to ABTA, the trade association.

However, all the major multiple agencies have now long abandoned that policy and follow a very strict line, not only as to which product to sell but, more importantly, which ones actively to promote. There is such massive duplication of product range within the travel trade that travel agents could, if they wished, cut out the majority of ABTA tour operators without undermining to any significant degree the quality and width of choice of holiday available to their potential customer. The advantages to the travel agent of such a policy significantly outweigh any occasional lost sale. Being more selective can ensure:

— A product range which is more compatible with overall image.
— Better product knowledge among staff, helping the maintenance of service standards.
— Differentiation with competitors.
— Stronger purchasing power.

Whether travel agents restrict product range or not, many of them still determine their product choice by the level of percentage commission they can earn on a booking. As the industry grows up and falls more in line with the proven marketing methods of mainstream non-travel retailers, this will change. More will follow the current market leaders and base product range decisions on their strategic market positioning. A controlled product range is part and parcel of the increasing segmentation of the retail trade and the range must reflect the marketing position any travel retailer is taking.

To retailers outside the travel industry, this idea of restricting product range is, of course, far from unusual, not least because it is physically impossible not to! Every other shop in the high street does it and the shopper is quite used to not finding a total range of products in any one particular shop. The travel agent should be no different, either in the owners' or the customers' eyes.

Price

The principal sets the price of the product and the agent takes a percentage commission. This is, and has been, the basic tenet of travel agency business throughout the world. But price competition has crept up on the industry and is about to explode upon the scene. The leisure travel business, in the UK in particular, is about to enter a phase of concentrating on price discount — just as the business travel sector has done over the past five years. There will be a fixation on how much the travel agency can cut the cost of a holiday for the customer.

There are increasing examples of the breakdown of the current price regime. Not only are special fares being negotiated by travel agents with airlines, but special packages are being put together in the leisure air sector, allowing travel agents to build up price differential. If the changes in the airline/travel agent relationship represent evolution, then that potentially about to hit the tour operator/travel agents relationship in the UK is revolutionary and could have reverberations across the world wherever there is a package holiday market. In the UK the tour operators' right to dictate price has been referred to the Monopolies and Mergers Commission, where the decision went against them. In 1984 and 1985 travel agents faced falling volumes and non-travel retailers looking to discounts on travel as a way of bolstering failing sectors of their business. This led to dramatic breaches of the existing 'no discounting', clauses in principals/agency agreements. In many cases, this was done by quasi-discounting through offers such as free insurance, free transport to the airport and discounts on other products in the shop. But increasingly there have been examples of straight discounting by the travel agent, particularly as some tour operators do not put any restrictions on discounting in their agency agreements.

The decision to outlaw those remaining clauses which do maintain the tour operator's right to control price will have major consequences on the way the industry is structured; consequences similar to those experienced in the grocery industry in the UK when resale price maintenance was removed — initial major price competition and ultimately a change of power from the manufacturer to the major multiple retailers and purchasing groups. While the pace of the travel industry's transition may differ, because travel agencies hold no stock and therefore have much less flexibility of margin, there is no doubt that price competition would mobilise the multiple chains into completely reviewing their product range policy. It could lead to them actively planning to manufacture or package their own products, taking major pre-season commitments and increasing their risk. This may be the only way they will be able to protect their margins and still be price competitive. Aggressive price competition would also accelerate the development of own brand products as a further way of providing differentiation, both in price and product range. Thomas Cook's decision to bring their tour operation totally in-house, available only through its own shops, is just the first step in this trend.

In short, any decision to allow unfettered price competition would ride straight against the whole concept of principal/agency relationships and could catapult the UK holiday travel business into a new era requiring new decision variables and new skills within the retail sector. Many companies will not be able to cope with the shock.

Staff And Service Levels

Staff numbers and quality are fundamental to any service industry. The travel agency sector is no exception. Of all the management skills required by the business, the management of staff has arguably the greatest impact on profitability. Even more than most high street retailers, travel agents are not simply selling products, they are selling service. Holidays are an emotive purchase, made even more so by the fact that money has to be handed over prior to the product being seen; they also represent one of the biggest, if not the biggest, purchase of the year. On top of that, they are ephemeral.

The role of travel agents in the decision-making process varies enormously. Some customers know what they want and simply want the travel agent to book: however, increasingly customers are coming to travel agents with a set of broad criteria and are expecting them not only to provide a range of products but also advice and information. While shop location, layout, advertising and product range may tempt the customer into the shop, it has traditionally been the level of service and the ability to get the right product to the right customer that have converted the customers into business and brought them back again the following year. Travel agents, like all retailers, rely on repeat business.

Good service has a number of components but staff are still central. Yet while service can be the secret to profit, mismanagement of staffing levels can be the guarantee of loss.

At one extreme, payroll can represent as high as 80% of total costs, and certainly will equal anything from 35 to 60% of a travel agency's total revenue, whether that travel agent is a multiple or an independent. Furthermore, the sale of much of the leisure travel product requires skilled staff, skilled not only in selling techniques but also in terms of product knowledge, booking procedures and how to obtain and interpret ancillary information required by the customer.

The degree of skill required will inevitably depend on the market position taken by the travel agent. Those that simply aim to sell package holidays require less product and knowledge skills. It is clearly their policy to look for cheaper, less technically capable staff, but with a good sales manner. Cheaper staff are accompanied by lower training costs.

On the other hand, full service travel agents, particularly if they are dealing with such products as worldwide rail and complicated air fare constructions, have to contemplate a different staffing structure and substantial training costs in order to maintain their service levels across their product range. It is no coincidence that a number of the larger UK multiples have decided to concentrate on package holidays and have withdrawn other service-intensive products.

The management of staff is complicated further by the seasonality of the retail holiday business in the UK, and the move towards seven-day trading;

both phenomena have been, or will be, tackled by goods retailers through the introduction of temporary or weekend staff. This solution is less easily available to service retailers, especially given the rapidly increasing speed of change in the products being sold and the rising expectations of customers. There are no ready-made answers to these issues, but failure to think them through could mean loss not only of market share but profit.

The psychology of a customer buying leisure travel is not fundamentally different from a customer buying other high value durables. In that respect travel is irrelevant; it is simply the product sold. While the particular demands of this product do create specific problems, the general issues are still those which face the traditional retailer. At a strategic level there are more lessons to be learnt from the action and history of other high street retailers than from the travel industry itself. In most areas, travel agents are far enough behind not to have to worry too much about innovation — simply catching up would generate great improvement. A few travel agents have already shown how effective this policy is in improving their business and profitability.

Travel agents cannot afford to allow the financial and legal arguments around the principal/agency relationship to distract them. Even if the trade think they are agents, customers will judge them as retailers.

The Challenges Of The Future

While the independent travel agents may well be entering the last phase of their retail life cycle, the multiples have still some way to go before they plateau. There are still many threats and problems to overcome if they are to prevent their total business being undermined during that period.

The threats facing the business travel agent and the leisure travel agent are different but they stem from the same two sources — the consumer and technology, either working together or separately. Increasing consumer sophistication and knowledge do present a direct threat to the travel agent: a business traveller knowing more about his needs than the travel agents and being able to book direct; the leisure traveller growing in confidence and demanding more individuality in the holiday arrangements and overcoming the psychological demand for face to face contact in the purchase. And while these particular pressures are building on the industry, the travel agent will have to cope with the wider changes being faced by all corporate suppliers and high street retailers.

All corporate suppliers are having to face the changing structure of industry: the move in western countries away from the manufacturing base into the faster moving, less predictable high technology/service industrial base. This is combined with increasing changes in management style: a growth in multinationals but also a realisation of local accountability. Business travel agents, therefore, are having to face the demand to provide service and control mechanisms to their corporate customers' central headquarters, while at the same time providing an image and service which satisfy the demands and increasing self-determination of the corporations' individual profit centres, both in the base country and overseas. They will have to work with increasingly complicated international communication and payment systems and a volatile trading environment.

The leisure travel agents, from whatever developed country, will find themselves embroiled within the problems facing every retailer; for example, increasing demands by customers for different and longer trading hours, demands for higher standards of service and specialisation. They will have to make decisions on shop location: should they move out of town, should they concentrate their resources into small local units or build up big, impressive central high street/precinct operations? They will also have decisions to make on products. Do they continue to provide a wide range, do they specialise, what percentage of their business should be own brand and should they diversify into different but related product ranges?

Those who preach the demise of the travel agent point in particular to the impact new technology will have on the business. They point to the potential growth of self-ticketing machines; they point to home shopping and claim both as essentially cheaper and more effective distribution methods for suppliers. If technology was being ignored by the retail travel agent, then these prophets of doom would have some justification. So far this has not proved the case — technology is already being used by the retail travel agents as one of its strongest sources of power and development. While it may present threats, it also opens up the future.

So while the opportunities beckon, there are many obstacles in the path. To overcome them, travel agents will need to show greater depth and flexibility of management than have been evidenced in the past. Only that way will they cope with an environment where the accelerating rate of change in consumer demand and expectation is only matched by the accompanying rate of change in products and systems.

The Changing Customers

Holidays

Much is written about market segmentation in retailing. With this marketing theory dominating the retail sector, it cannot be ignored by the travel agency industry. Customers have growing expectations that specific selling messages will be made to them and are increasingly dissatisfied with mass packaging, particularly in such fashionable and image-orientated sectors as travel. This does not mean that the travel industry will be returning quickly to 'individual' holidays. This interpretation of the trend is misconceived. The 'individual' market will continue to exist and will expand somewhat but it is not the volume market of the near future, irrespective of the opportunities technology brings. What the previous mass non-discriminating marketing approach increasingly requires is not bespoke goods but group/life-style identity.

The travel agency sector has to decide how it is going to cope with segmentation. While the holiday manufacturers have recognised the trend and issued a wide range of brochures to meet different needs, few travel retailers have actively and deliberately positioned themselves to appeal to certain life-style sectors. This cannot continue. The failure of the travel agency industry to address this change in customer perceptions will have major and damaging impact on the industry's viability in two ways. On the one hand, the customer's perception of travel agencies, as against other retailers, will remain low and perhaps even diminish further as they fail to see shop profiles directed at them. On the other hand, travel agents face the very real threat of intervention by existing non-travel retailers.

It is this latter threat which is the most potentially damaging in the UK for the travel agent's holiday business. Travel is a very attractive ancillary product to other retailers. For high volume convenience stores, it raises their profile, helps them offer a complete service and can bring in marginal additional revenue. The strong interest, over the past 15 years, of department stores in having a travel operation is being complemented by the introduction of travel in a significant way into the out-of-town grocery superstores. The latter recognises the large element of convenience in the holiday purchase and the fact that, in most cases, the holiday purchase requires three or four visits to the place of booking. While it is still to be seen how profitable travel is within this environment, it does have the advantage of recognising and countering the difficulties currently experienced in purchasing travel on the high street, such as hours of opening and parking. With the high correlation of working couples with holiday-taking, the very convenience of these grocery superstores may overcome some of their environmental/design disadvantages for the travel product. Should grocery superstores begin to use travel and holidays as a marketing element of their mix rather than a major profit earner, then existing travel agents' positions will be severely threatened. Holidays undoubtedly have a strong emotional appeal and there will be growing use of holidays as a method of generating business in other sectors.

This potential threat to the existing industry may be greatest from the life-style retailers. There is no doubt that in many life-style segments of the population, holidays are a major part of their fashion/image purchases. Not only could the existence of travel in a shop enhance the overall life-style image but also provide cross-promotional opportunities. The business also has the extra value of having a customer flow/booking phasing which complements, in Europe at least, the traditional retail peaks.

There are a number of ways travel agents can counter these incursions from the non-travel sector. The increasing segmentation and complication of the market may, in itself, become a disincentive for other sectors, even if the existing low margins are not. Travel agents must find a way of showing that they can add value to a product and not simply be a booking agent for already packaged products. Furthermore, this must be done in a way which increases cost of entry. One of the reasons why the industry is occasionally raided by people from the outside is that the cost of entry is relatively low, both in terms of capital and risk. Increasing complexity, segmentation and value added products and also increasing technology may combine not only to improve the service and attraction of the trade but to provide better defences against attacks from outside.

Business Travel

While it may be relatively easy to accept that segmentation has relevance in the leisure market, it is surprising how hard it is for many travel agents to accept that it can also be applied to business travel. As was made clear earlier, there is no such thing as the corporate customer. Instead there is a whole range of different corporate customers with different servicing needs, often in the same organisation. This segmentation is almost bound to increase and it needs delicate but determined management to be able to bridge the differences and yet not completely undermine profitability.

Travel agents have to find completely different messages and products for different types of corporate customer. The large multinational has very different needs from the small local company. The large multinational manufacturing company will have different needs to an international city institution. Both of these will have different needs again from a partnership. As in the leisure market, while the base product will be the same, all of these customers will increasingly require identifiably different packaging.

So while the major multiple travel agents compete hard for large international corporate accounts, then their message becomes increasingly irrelevant for a local company. The multiples' product mix of central, but geographically distant, ticketing and servicing units, cheap fares, high technology, and business rebates do not have that great an appeal for a local businessman where reliability, service and individual attention are paramount. Nor does it have much relevance to the unstructured companies where the cultures and values would rule against central control of travel spend, this area being one where the executives are deliberately given freedom to make their own arrangements. This corporate customer may well prefer a less technologically sophisticated service from a local company where he knows the manager, or an electronic reservation service which can be used directly by a secretary.

Already travel agents are taking up their position in the increasingly segmented market: at the one extreme American Express Travel Related Services geared to global travel management, encompassing not only business travel but the whole management of travel and entertainment expenditure, and at the other extreme leisure-based multiples or small independents offering local, individual service based on strong knowledge and involvement in the local community.

But the parallel with leisure segmentation does not end there. As the market segments and the travel agents' messages begin to look blurred, then there is a real danger of intervention by non-travel corporate suppliers. Dominant among these potential predators are the financial institutions and information providers who see travel as an important part of their marketing platform but for whom the potential profitability of their base businesses far outweighs any profit potential travel has. It is no coincidence that the three major business travel companies in the UK are owned by banking, financial and insurance companies.

Failure to recognise this increasing sophistication of corporate and leisure customers could well be the downfall, if not of the travel agency sector as a whole, then at least of some of the existing major players within it. The greatest strategic mistake that can be made by travel agents now would be to believe that they can be all things to all people and that they should not discriminate as to the business they seek and take.

The Advance In Technology

Holidays

Retail travel agents may well be behind other high street retailers in many fields, but they are some way ahead in the use of technology and in particular information technology. It is arguably one of the most technologically sophisticated segments of the retail sector. Systems already exist in the UK which allow travel agents direct access to the computers of nearly all their major principals, between 80% and 90% of their total business. This direct access, using viewdata technology, allows them to search their principal's database, provide the customer with relevant choices, take out options, make bookings and confirm reservations.

Technology will create change but with that change come opportunities — opportunities to make major changes in the key decision areas discussed earlier.

Shop Location

Technology will affect shop location not least because it opens up new forms of distribution. While high street shops have a relatively secure future for the next 10 years, the holiday business is a prime candidate for home shopping.

But home shopping need not be the province of the manufacturer. It has far more potential as a method of distribution for the retailer. Customers still require advice, choice, comparisons and ancillary products, whether they are at the end of a computer or on the other side of the counter. Even so it is too easy to become convinced that the computer will devour the high street. The size of the customer's purchase and the psychological concerns surrounding it will mean that this form of direct sell is unlikely to take anything like the major share of the business this side of 2000.

Shop Design

If travel agents simply are booking agents and remain boring and office-like, then direct sell through technology may establish itself quicker. But technology itself provides salvation. For instance, the sophisticated use of video can overcome the problems of lack of in-store products. Initial experiments may have failed, but some of the multi-screen videos linked to reservation terminals or self-service systems currently on trial, will revolutionise shop layout and design among the mainstream travel retailers.

New technology in merchandising and shopfitting will allow retailers to change not only the packaging of their shops, but their whole nature, as they attempt to make the booking of a holiday as pleasurable as the anticipation of the holiday itself.

Product Range

There are a number of paths technology can take the travel retailer along in the provision of products. It already allows the salesperson to speed up the identification of potential products; it will not be long before expert systems are developed and the customer encouraged to go through the process of decision-making in a self-service mode within the branch. In time it will provide the opportunity for the travel industry to turn full circle and for more independent travel arrangements to re-establish their position in the marketplace. Technology will allow some of the task of matching beds and seats to revert to the travel agency — away from the tour operator. More immediate, and important, will be the greater opportunity to provide flexibility and improve the consumer/product match.

Price

Price has already been identified as one of the major potential catalysts for change in the industry. Should price control be loosened, then multiple retailers must look to enhance margins. The most likely way of doing this will be through purchase and control of stock. This can only be done effectively through the use of sophisticated stock control and direct reservations systems; i.e. converting the technology that is being developed by tour operators to the retailers' needs.

This move towards more traditional stock-holding retailing is already happening, with major retailers taking out substantial commitments to airline seats. It will not be long before the retailers expand this beyond seats into major upfront commitments to package holidays. This will open up not only the opportunity for new product ranges but completely new retail pricing structures.

Staff And Service Levels

The introduction of technology into the retail shop clearly has major implications for staffing, notably in terms of skills and in the balance between sales and administration personnel. As in most businesses, the real impact of technology in terms of organisation headcount will come in the support services to the shop or distribution outlet. The impact on the front-end staff will be less quantitative than qualitative. Technology will be used to enhance or substitute knowledge skills, by providing in the short term quick and easy access to static information and in the longer term by capturing choice-making skills within expert systems. Many multiple retailers already have large independent databases providing travel and product information. Research into expert systems is already under way and prototypes are being built and tested.

All this development does not necessarily mean that travel sales staff will not be required. What it does imply is that, over the long term, staff in high street shops will need less detailed memory of travel facts and more selling skills to identify and satisfy customers' real needs.

Not surprisingly, nothing is black or white; for as many threats technology presents to the leisure travel agent, there are opportunities: opportunities to break away from the dull office-based booking function which has become the bread and butter of the business for travel agents in Northern Europe. Technology is primarily a tool with which the travel retailer can improve the message and service to the customer. But it is also recognised outside the travel agency sector as a way of blazing a new distribution trail. It will be up to the leisure travel agent to fight these predators off — their existing trading format may not survive but, making the proper use of technology, they should be able to retain control of the link with the customer.

Business Travel

Technology has made a far greater and quicker impact on the business travel market than it has on leisure travel. The extensive use of computers and international communication systems by airlines has been the backbone of this development and most serious business travel agents will have automated reservations, ticketing, invoice and statement printing and data capture. On top of this are the technological links with financial payment systems, as pointed out in Roger Hymas's chapter.

Technology plays a much more central role in business travel than it does in leisure. It is this fact, plus the far greater sophistication of the customer, that means that technology does present a far greater threat in this sector. It is not an insuperable threat, but travel agents will have to move quickly to ensure that their position in the market is strong and protected if they are not going to find major sectors of their business bypassed. The systems which travel agents use are primarily airline based. It is technically perfectly feasible for these systems to be further developed to provide automated ticketing at airports, direct access by customers or distribution through other non-travel agent outlets. Indeed in many cases such systems already exist — the technology is there, it is simply a matter of whether the proposition presentable to the customer direct through technology has greater appeal than that presented through the travel agent. It also depends on whether the potential volume through this route makes it worthwhile for an airline to risk undermining its relationship with its current prime base of business.

There are two directions of the technology threat to the travel agency's business: the use of the reservation system direct by the corporate customer and the encroachment into the business by information providers as they move from hard copy to electronic publishing. The threat is greatest in those environments where airfares are deregulated and travel agency purchasing power cannot obtain special rates not generally available on the market. It is not surprising, therefore, that the major developments in this field have been in the USA, where the large proportion of domestic traffic, coupled with deregulation, has presented major opportunities for both the systems and information suppliers.

The travel agent may lose the 'do as told' business traveller because this highly centralised corporate organisation may move to having reservation and ticketing facilities on site, linked into a payment and control system which ensures that the cheapest and most appropriate fares are provided for the executive. Even if security or regulatory restrictions prevent the ticketing taking place on site in some countries, the travel agent to this corporate client risks being relegated to the role of the ticketing and ancillary service provider, with little or no control over the purchasing decision and, therefore, with much reduced power in relation to the airlines.

Travel agents risk losing the 'do as allowed' or 'do it yourself' business traveller as these find that they can make a reservation through their desk top personal computer and that this service is provided free of charge by airlines or one of the corporate information providers. This personal freedom, particularly if accompanied by the enticements of frequent flyer programmes, will again relegate the travel agent to a ticketing agency, if that. The prime motivating factor towards a consumer using such systems is convenience: a fact that travel agents can easily underestimate, as they tend to build more and more complex products and services.

The investment and development of the two main airline fares and timetable publishers (OAG and ABC) are watched with interest and some trepidation by travel agents and airlines alike. There is little or no doubt that they have the opportunity to take significant sectors of the business in certain parts of the world.

Meanwhile, the multiple, international, travel agents are busy developing ways of harnessing technology to their needs to provide the value added service that will fight off technology-based direct sell. International and national communication networks are being developed, allowing for a transmission of up-to-date information, the distribution of price-sensitive products and the enhancement of customer service; this is accompanied by the building up of ancillary products such as airport services, hotel reservations, management information and travel and expenses control systems — all of which the new competitors will find difficult to match. And if individual travel agencies cannot develop these themselves, they are creating international consortia to do so for them.

Again, technology provides threats and opportunities; but the pace of change in the business travel market is far quicker than in the leisure business and the short and medium term threats to the traditional travel agent method of doing business are far greater. Business travel is becoming a business that fewer and fewer travel agents are being able to afford to undertake, certainly when you are dealing with major international corporations. The rationalisation of this business in the UK and North America is well under way, whereas the rationalisation of leisure travel retailers has only recently begun.

Technology creates opportunity for change. But if the basis of the business is to change fundamentally, it will not be driven by technology but by the customer. Brilliant technological opportunities will not work unless the customer understands and is interested in the end product. The battle for distribution is a battle for the customer's heart and mind and there is a real danger that technology will move too far ahead of both of them.

Technology's partner is complication, a sort of technological version of Parkinson's law; give somebody a computer with 400 characteristics and he will feel he has to use all of them. Such complication leads to confusion and confusion leads to the need for guidance to the consumer and hence a role for the retailer. In the days before computers, no airline would have contemplated having over 20 different fare structures on one flight — now it is possible. Multiply that by the number of flights and the number of airlines, then it becomes unlikely that a consumer will feel confident that, in going direct to one airline, he or she will get the best deal. As technology allows the principals to make their products more complicated in their attempt to increase yield and avoid becoming a commodity, so technology will help the retailers in their role of making things simpler, providing relevant value for money choice for the consumer.

One thing is certain, and that is that survival in all sectors of the market will require significant investment in technology. The difference between the two sectors may be that outsiders will provide the technology to support the leisure travel agent, but the travel agents themselves will have to provide the technology to support and develop and consolidate their position in business travel. Technology is already creating change; however, if its energy and power have been harnessed they are by no means expended.

Strategic Options

If these are the challenges facing travel retailers' managements, then existing companies, let alone those wishing to enter the business, have to come to terms with the consequences.

Traditionally the retail travel business has been seen as an easy one to enter, requiring little capital. Shops have been small and simple; there has been no stock to purchase; return on capital has been generally good. However, the changes envisaged in this chapter alter many past assumptions. As good leisure travel retailers move into prime high street sites offering a strong and sophisticated service, then it will become increasingly difficult for the poorly-located travel agent to survive. If good business travel retailers are investing heavily in new technology and communication systems then the 'back of the shop' business travel unit will have little to offer. Furthermore, if the travel retailer moves into taking stock, then all retail history indicates that volume will become vital to success — again reinforcing the need for prime locations, big portfolios and large branch networks. Finally, technology will require substantial investment by principal and retailer alike. All this means increased risk, greater committed funds and less attractive cash flow.

The business is rapidly moving from low to high cost of entry. Those who try to avoid these costs and still look for the same rosy return on capital that they have received in the past will find the future somewhat disillusioning. On the other hand, those retailers who seize the chance, take the risk and participate in the next quantum leap of the business, will find themselves in strong and to a large degree impregnable positions, impregnable at least from other travel agents. They will also find themselves with the purchasing power and the profit to ensure that they can secure their future as the market changes through the customer and technology.

Whether the travel agent is rising to power or falling from grace will be a matter of opinion. What is clear is that they start the race for the hearts and minds of the customers of the 1990s better placed than they were a decade ago, and, in many countries, in poll position.

At the time of writing **Luke Mayhew** from New Zealand was Director of Retailing at Thomas Cook's with wide responsibilities for the development of the company's future strategy in that area. Prior to this he was a senior civil servant in the Department of Trade and Industry. Luke is now with British Airways assisting in that organisation's redevelopment and structural growth.

5

The Development Of Travel Related Insurance Protection And Its Role In The Growth Of The Travel Market

INTRODUCTION
In this chapter we shall review the role that insurance has played in supporting the growth of the travel industry. We shall look at the viewpoint of

the buyers — who seek protection
the sellers — who earn commission
the regulators — who set the rules
the underwriters — who take the risks

We shall highlight the importance of insurance in protecting the cash flow of travel companies and travellers. We shall show that, without the financial strength of the insurance industry, the travel industry would have developed more slowly and many independents would have been unable to enter, and survive, at least without much higher inputs of capital.

1. BACKGROUND

During the last 10–15 years we have seen a massive growth in international travel both for business and holiday purposes, due to:

— increasing living standards;
— a vast growth in airline capacity;
— an organised growth of bulk purchasing, reducing unit costs for the individual;
— a rapid growth in international trade and cross border investment.

The result is that every year millions of people leave home to sample new cultures and environments; taking their belongings with them; experiencing new foods, dealing with the stresses of travel and its potential dislocations and investing relatively large sums of money, often many weeks prior to departure.

In particular increased vacation time, occupational pensions, longer life expectancy, and cheap off-peak travel and accommodation have resulted in an explosion of travel by the over 50s. This growth has raised an increasing problem of dealing with illness and accidents and with the funding of medical care and/or repatriation. Most tourists economies have not invested in the development of medical care to support the growth of visitors. Many travellers, especially those from Europe, come from economies in which medical care is not personally funded and therefore have little perception of its true cost, until they are faced with having to buy it overseas. Even visitors who are used to paying for it at home do not realise the limits on their coverage when travelling.

In overall terms, the system has coped very well. However, as numbers have risen there have inevitably been problems due to human error, over-stretch (physical and financial) and plain dishonesty. Large volumes of people from better off societies, intent on personal pleasure, visiting less privileged environments with underdeveloped infrastructures were bound to result in sickness, accidents, theft, exploitation and disappointment.

Many of the companies participating in this growth were new, were experiencing rapid growth on a small capital base and therefore failed their customers or their financial backers, leaving behind a trail of claims/litigation and disappointment. During the growth phase, rules were made to favour the suppliers because the public were getting deals much better than they could ever achieve on their own, or by staying in their own country. Consequently, tour operators and travel agents have been able to insist on substantial up-front payments which, in effect, become part of their working capital, especially as it has not been common practice to require them to separate their customers' funds from their own. This process has created severe risks for the customer, both from:

a) his inability to travel as he had planned, due to any number of legitimate reasons;

b) the bankruptcy of the agent and/or tour operator or airline losing his money, or not being able to provide him with the contracted service and/or leaving him stranded.

These threats were exacerbated by excessive competition when growth in supply outran demand. This imbalance resulted in dramatic failures such as Clarkson's, Court Line, Braniff, Continental and many small, less publicised events.

Against the background painted, it is not surprising that the need arose, and an opportunity existed, for the insurance industry to deal with these problems. It has certainly met the challenge and travel-related insurance is now a large, well-developed segment in each major market.

The travel industry recognised very early that the most convenient point for buying insurance was when booking travel, and that it could make substantial revenues from such sales. It has pursued the opportunity aggressively and its various parties now compete vigorously to increase their share of the cake.

In the following sections, we shall look in some detail at the key role which insurance has played in the development of the travel market. Without the support of insurance, travel industry funding would have needed to be organised differently and certainly would have required more capital input by the many who have profited greatly from the growth of this vast industry.

2. The Buyers' View

Personal Protection

The key principle of insurance is that the many fund the losses of the few. From an individual viewpoint, the payment of a premium is a means of protecting against an unforeseen catastrophe severely threatening financial stability. However, at the same time, money spent on insurance is negative expenditure unless an incident occurs which requires a claim to be made. Therefore people wish to spend the least possible, and will spend nothing unless they have a clear perception that there is a risk which they could not deal with from their own resources: this means that insurance has to be sold.

In the travel area the public do now understand the risks and some 90% + of those taking inclusive tours buy insurance. Substantial credit for this must go to the travel industry and its trade associations, who have worked hard to create this position. On the other hand, only about 60% of those making their own arrangements purchase coverage and, therefore, there is still a substantial number of people at risk. Statistics show that on average between five and six travellers in each hundred make a claim of some kind and, therefore, those not buying insurance are taking a substantial risk.

Credibility of Suppliers

In the mind of the consumer, the existence of insurance supports the credibility of the supplier, in that it extends his capital base in one of two ways. Namely,

— if he purchases insurance it helps him meet claims without adversely affecting his cash flow, e.g. insuring his aircraft against loss and third party liability;
— if his customer purchases insurance it enables him to establish terms of business which are more favourable to him, while reducing the

likelihood of having arguments with his customer, e.g. requiring the customer to pay cancellation charges.

It may be said that the above is more to the benefit of the supplier than the customer. However, if problems arise the consumer has the confidence that he has somewhere to go to get paid, and it is this security that he is seeking.

Funding Specialist Services

The existence of a large insured-customer base enables expensive specialist services to be funded cost effectively. These services, by their very nature, will be required relatively infrequently. An excellent example of this is the medical repatriation facility for the seriously ill/injured traveller. This facility has become a standard element of insurance coverage in many countries over the last five years. The cost can be as much as £10,000 per incident but, spread over many people, is purchased for a few pence per head. A review of some of the tragic accidents that have been dealt with highlights the value of such a facility to the unfortunate few.

A similar benefit is ensuring the availability of special medical care in the country being visited, and the existence of a financial guarantee to fund expenses. This aspect is particularly vital in the USA where treatment costs can escalate alarmingly from long stay care and where a guaranteed means of payment is vital to personal security.

3. The Sellers' View

Channels of Distribution

The dominant sales channels for travel insurance are tour operators and travel agents. Others include insurance brokers, credit card companies, banks and direct sell underwriters (either via mass marketing or through their own agency force). The balance varies in each country, depending on the relative importance of inclusive tours. If we take the UK, for example, the broad picture is as follows:

Inclusive Tours:	
Tour Operator Schemes	60%
Retail Agents Schemes	35%
Others	5%
	100%

90% of these sales are through travel agents who earn commissions for selling the tour operator schemes and who, therefore, are responsible for some 90% of total sales.

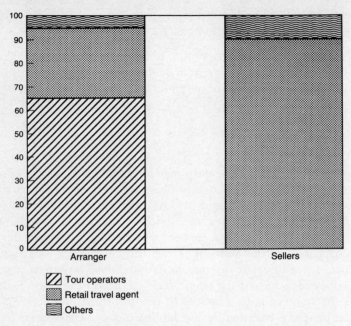

FIG. 5.1. Market share analysis, inclusive tours (U.K.).

Other Holiday Trips:

Retail Travel Agents	60%
Others	40%
	100%

Business Travel

The insurance of business travellers is not well documented, but it is believed that it is dominated by insurance brokers who arrange cover as part of the overall corporate programme. Travel agents who attempt to sell business travel packages have not been successful, as in general they have not provided a competitive alternative.

By comparison, in Australia the travel agent schemes are much more dominant.

Travel Agent Schemes	80%
Tour Operator Schemes	15%
Other	5%
	100%

The main reason for this difference is the lower incidence of inclusive tour arrangements.

The key reason for the travel agent's domination is the convenience

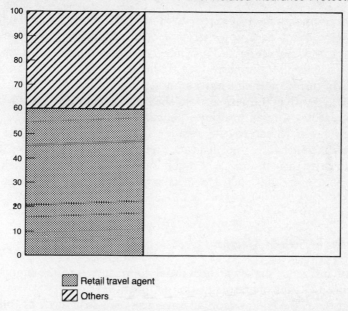

Retail travel agent
Others

FIG.5.2. Market share analysis, other holiday trips (U.K.).

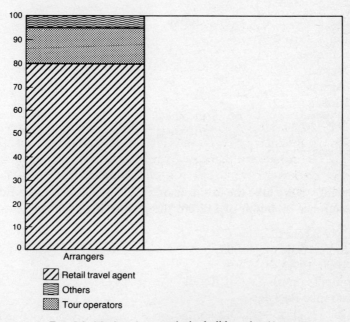

Arrangers

Retail travel agent
Others
Tour operators

FIG. 5.3. Market share analysis, holiday trips (Australia).

element of purchasing insurance with the booking. Travel agents unfortunately do not have any well developed technical expertise and/or highly developed marketing skills. The growing importance of multiple travel agents is resulting in more investment in training and promotional skills. This in turn is putting pressure on the tour operators' market share for, as will be shown in the next section, the travel agent earns a much better return from selling a retail insurance package.

The continuous threat to the retailer is the possibility of the tour operator/airline including the insurance in their package and/or being prepared to offer their insurance at much lower prices by cutting their own margin. There is certainly a trend in this direction from the credit card companies.

Contribution of Seller's Margin

The sale of insurance makes a substantial contribution to the margins of travel agents and tour operators at the net profit level.

In broad terms the commission arrangements are structured as follows:

	Retail Schemes	Tour Operator Schemes
Premium paid by Traveller	100%	100%
Commission Received by		
Arranging Broker	0–10%	0–5%
Tour Operator	—	40–50%
Travel Agents Association	0–5 %	—
Travel Agent	30–40%	10%
Total	40–50%	50–60%
Premium Received by Underwriter	50–60%	40–50%

Consequently if we take the example of a £200 inclusive tour to Europe, with an insurance premium of £12.00, the picture is as follows:

Retail Travel Agent		
Commission on Sale of Holiday (Assume basic 10%)	£20	
a) Commission on Sale of Retail Insurance Package	£4–5	
% increase in income from selling retail insurance	+ 20–25%	

b)	Commission on sale Tour Operator's insurance	£1.2
	% increase in income from selling Tour Operator's insurance	+6%

Tour Operator
Net Margin on Holiday   £10
(Assume 5%)

a)	Commission if Agent sells his insurance	£5
	% increase in margin	+50%
b)	Commission if Agent sells retail insurance	–
	% increase in margin	–

The above figures show clearly the degree of dynamic tension that exists within the market-place due to the conflicting interests of the principals and their distribution networks. In the UK alone the overall premium is estimated to be some £200 million and therefore a commission income of £80–100 million is being fought for.

A very significant Risk Transfer

We referred earlier to the way in which insurance can be used by travel organisations to lay off their own risks, thereby protecting their balance sheets and income statements. This is no different in many ways from any business enterprise, i.e. using insurance to protect against loss of assets through fire etc., against third party claims, employee error/dishonesty and so on.

However, there are some special exposures where insurance has been extremely beneficial. For example:

Tour Operators/Airlines

a) Cancellation
   Travellers cancelling prior to departure forfeit their advance payments/ deposits. The costs of so doing are met by insurers. This process releases the seat, thereby enabling the operator/airline to resell it if demand allows and at worst protects his original revenue.

b) Travel Delay
   Tour operators charge holidaymakers an amount in their administration charges to provide certain benefits in the event of their being delayed for

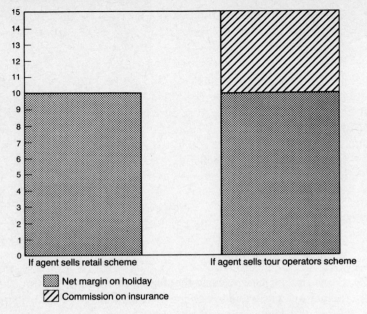

FIG.. 5.4. Increase in margin of tour operator.

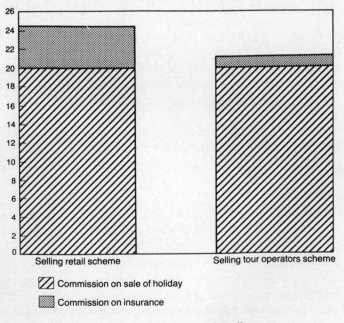

FIG. 5.5. Increase in margin of retail agent.

reasons such as strikes, bad weather. This risk is then laid off in the insurance market, often for a much lower amount than that charged to the traveller.

c) Strikes at Hotels

Some policies provide payments for the unavailability of facilities at hotels, due to strikes. This helps to reduce consumer dissatisfaction and the likelihood of the operator having to make amends in some way.

Travel Agents

a) Tour Operator Failure

The provision of cover to the traveller in the event of the tour operator failing is certainly very helpful to the booking agent in that his clients' money is recovered from a third party with the ability to pay.

b) The existence of cancellation cover benefits agents by returning money to their clients to be spent at a later date and also releasing a seat which can be resold through the system.

The above are only some of the ways in which insurance aids the financial viability of the travel industry. As exposures change, we would expect the insurance industry to offer innovations to meet the needs of one of the world's largest, and fastest-growing industries.

4. The Regulations View

Regulatory arrangements and conditions vary greatly in the developed countries, which generate the majority of the world's travellers. In principle there are two levels of interest, namely:

— Governments themselves;
— Regulatory bodies for the travel industry at government level.

In broad terms, governments are interested in :

— improving consumer protection;
— reducing embarrassing dislocations;
— arranging for others to finance catastrophes;
— weighing the scales in favour of their own national interests.

These motivations exist vis-a-vis both the travel and insurance industries.

The insurance industry's role is mainly as a provider of finance to meet losses, whether it be of national airlines, investors in tourist facilities, or the public. While this process goes on smoothly, there is little intervention. It is when the insurance industry finds it unattractive to meet the needs at a price which is acceptable, relative to the risks, that governments tend to involve themselves. Normally this involvement is the result of some set of circumstances which have caused loss of life or money to the public, e.g. the bankruptcy of a major travel operator, or the inadequacy of fire regulations in hotels and public places. The extension of legislation to meet such circumstances normally creates new opportunities for the insurance industry, in that one group's obligations to another are publicly broadened, thereby creating a risk which needs financing and for which someone is now willing to pay.

Travel Trade Regulatory Bodies

The travel industry has grown to be very important and operates very much in the public eye. Consequently it has placed great stress in establishing effective self-regulatory mechanisms. In broad terms these tend to represent either the providers, e.g. IATA, or the sellers, e.g. ABTA, ASTA. However, because of the extent of vertical integration and a substantial degree of mutual self interest, the travel agents associations in some countries tend to represent both providers and sellers, for example, ABTA; and attempt to find internal means of dealing with conflicts of interest such as the establishment within ABTA of a Tour Operators' Council and a Retail Agents' Council. The key to maintaining the maximum degree of freedom to self-regulate is to be seen to be dedicated to consumer protection, and to deal effectively with breakdowns in the system. Any resulting restrictions to free trade are often then accepted as a necessary price of protecting the public, and will remain until some new solution is found, or the restriction itself becomes untenable and is amended or removed by competitive pressure.

Travel industry bodies recognised very early on, and very sensibly, that the vast capital base of the insurance industry could be very helpful to meet losses, finance dislocations/catastrophes, and to provide substantial income to themselves and their members. They positively encouraged the purchase of insurance by their customers and applied considerable pressure to expand and improve coverage and to keep down premiums. One measure of their success is that many people are much better insured while travelling than they are in their normal daily life. There is, without a doubt, an important marketing lesson here for the insurance industry.

As the travel insurance market has matured, and the growth in new customers slowed, with increased levels of penetration, competition has become extreme and underwriting losses have risen to unacceptable levels. The travel industry has traditionally shown little concern for the financial returns of underwriters as it sought to achieve higher commissions and more coverage without premium increases. It now has to deal with that reality, as underwriters begin to take a tougher line and/or remove themselves from the business.

5. The Underwriters' View

Financial Results

During the last five years, there has been one consistent trend for underwriters of travel business throughout the world. Results have deteriorated to such an extent that it is not uncommon to be paying out between 20 and 40% more money than premiums received. A good performance would be that losses equal premiums minus expenses.

There are many reasons for this trend, namely:
— increases in coverage have not been matched by adequate additional premiums;
— claims costs have risen due to a higher incidence and a rising average payment;
— plentiful reinsurance capacity encouraged new entrants to buy their way into the market;
— commission levels to attempt to improve market share.

In principle, all the above are reflections of an extremely competitive market. Without doubt the buyers and sellers have had an excellent run, but times are now changing. In the last twelve months there have been many examples of a tightening market. If the consumer really wants the levels of coverage that he has become used to, he will have to pay more premium or meet more of the losses at the lower end through increased deductibles.

Analysis of claims

In the last three or four years much more importance has been given to improving claims statistics, so as to get a better picture of the pattern of losses, thereby aiding more sophisticated pricing, and target marketing better than average consumer groups. In broad terms the British experience can be summarised as below:

I) Analysis by Type of Loss

	% of Total losses
Accident	2%
Medical Expenses	30–40%
Lost Baggage/Money	20–30%
Cancellation/Curtailment	25–40%
Other	5–10%
	100%

Other includes — travel delay, liability, tour operator failure, etc.

It is clear that there are three major areas of significance, i.e. medical, baggage/money, cancellation. The relative importance of these varies mainly with consumer group characteristics, for example,

— Medical expenses are higher for older travellers on extended trips
— Cancellation is higher in areas where redundancy is above average

These figures show the major role played by the insurance industry in financing cancellations and therefore in supporting the present booking/payment system.

II) Incidence Rates

In total some 5–6 people out of every hundred make a claim, broken down as follows:

	Incidence/100 Travellers
Personal Accident	0.01
Medical	1.5 – 2.5
Lost Baggage/Money	2
Cancellation/Curtailment	1
Other	0.5 – 1.0
	5–6

III) Average Claim Size

	£ Sterling
Personal Accident	na
Medical	350
Lost Baggage/Money	90
Cancellation/Curtailment	250
Other	—
Overall Average	160

IV) Control of Claims Costs
Controlling claims costs can be done in four main ways, namely:

— rejecting doubtful and/or fraudulent claims
— imposing an element of self insurance to remove small claims
— minimising the opportunity for suppliers of services to overcharge
— imposing ceilings and/or restrictions on coverage

By their very nature, these activities are unpopular and bring with them the threat of adverse publicity. However, they are vital if the overall costs to the public of buying protection are to be contained. In practice, because of the pressures that can be brought by consumers, the media, travel regulators

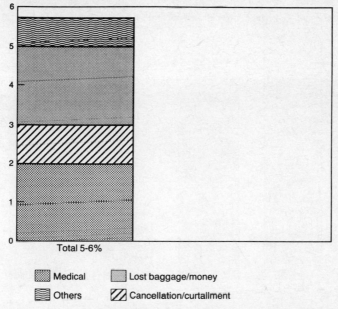

FIG. 5.6. Incidence of claims per 100 travellers.

and politicians, the balance is usually towards the consumer and this is unlikely to change.

Insurers and their specialist claims-handling organisations are vastly improving their statistical base, in order to be in a better position to achieve profitable results. However, in a free market their ability to capitalise on these data will depend on the overall supply and demand situations and in their ability to claw back premium from administrative and sales costs. We expect to see some major changes in the next few years.

6. Product Groups

Travel Packages

We have concentrated our attention on the package policies bought by travellers either on a per trip or annual basis, as this has been the fastest-growing area and the one which receives the highest profile. However, there are some other areas of insurance which play a vital part in securing the finances of the travel industry we should refer to, albeit briefly.

Financial Contingency/Guarantee Coverages

Financial bonding arrangements are an integral part of consumer protection in that they provide some protection to monies which are being passed over

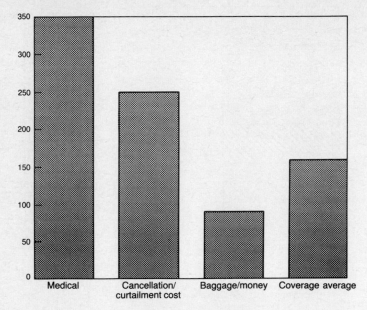

FIG. 5.7. Average size of claim.

to travel companies prior to the service being provided. They are also important in protecting one participant, an airline, say, from the failure of another, a travel agent. Insurance-based bonds also have the advantage that they remove the need to deposit scarce capital with a financial institution.

Asset Coverages

Insurance provides protection against the cost of replacing assets which are an integral part of operating the business, premises, aeroplanes, buses and so on. These coverages can also be extended to meet the revenue lost from the unavailability of the asset, a critical element in maintaining cash flow and therefore financial viability.

Liability Coverages

Travel companies are increasingly threatened by claims being made against them by third parties. The claimants can be the dependents of those killed by an incident; individuals who feel wronged and/or who are injured; other companies; shareholders. The reason may be professional incompetence and/or genuine errors. The result is the same in many courts — someone must pay.

Legislation has grown more complex, causing problems for the owners of small companies who cannot afford their own legal expert. The insurance industry has helped by providing legal advisory services, either as part of an insurance policy or as a stand alone service.

Liability exposures will continue to grow and insurance protection will become much more expensive, due to horrific losses made by underwriters. The result will be a growing expense item for travel companies, the alternative being substantial losses of shareholders' funds.

7. Development Of Travel Package Policies

Coverage

During the last five years the coverage provided by travel policies has expanded rapidly both in terms of amounts of cover and range of benefits.

The table below shows the scale of change in UK.

	1980	1985
Personal Accident		
Death	£2 – 5,000	£15,000
Permanent Disablement		£25,000
Medical Expenses	£5,000	£500,000–unlimited + Emergency Service
Baggage	£500	£1,000
Money	£100	£200
Cancellation	illness only	any cause beyond the control of the traveller

Additional benefits, such as failure of the operator or public transport, withdrawal of services by hotels, travel delay, hospitalisation benefits, have also been included. Similar trends have taken place in the USA, Australia, Japan. Many other exclusions and/or policy restrictions have been removed thereby increasing claims costs, e.g. pre-existing medical conditions.

Pricing

During the same five year period, average prices have increased by only 60–70% in money terms (i.e. allowing for inflation there has been little real increase). Consequently, the increases in benefits have not been charged for; the result to underwriters are those shown earlier.

Changes in pricing strategy have been introduced, to separate out different risk profiles, such as destinations — local, long haul, and length of stay — one week, two weeks, one month, longer. This process has certainly been helpful to underwriters but has not in itself been sufficient to bring about profitability.

One of the problems is that, because of the high commission levels, any increase in price to the underwriter costs the consumer twice as much. For this reason increasing deductibles (i.e. the amount of the claim paid by the traveller) has become a much more effective way of improving underwriters' financial performance. However, this approach is very unpopular with the buyers and the sellers and, therefore, emphasis is now being placed on reducing commission levels.

Geographical Spread

The package policy was initiated in the UK, but has now become common in most of the developed economies. National travel associations and their international equivalents such as UFTA (United Federation of Travel Agents) have certainly played a major role in its development.

In recent years the concept has been exported to many countries by international brokers who have provided the insurance, sales and administrative expertise necessary to launch the product. Such countries include Hong Kong, Philippines, Singapore, Malaysia, Spain, Latin America and Israel. We expect this development to continue.

Developments in the USA have been slower, due to the particular problems of insurance legislation in that country and the fact that certain aspects of the coverage are incorporated in other insurance policies. However, in the last three years substantial marketing investment has been made in expanding the concept and major new participants have entered the ring, notably, Blue Cross. In addition, credit card companies and travellers cheque vendors have placed great emphasis on marketing insurance protection as add-on-goodies.

8. Future Trends

Product Structures

Three issues are relevant to future product structures, namely:
— changes in the nature and/or size of risk exposures
— changes in the packaging of cover under the various policies
— financial results of underwriters

Exposure Pattern
We see the key risk areas remaining as medical, loss of baggage/money, cancellation and/or curtailment. Personal accident and third party liability coverages will be increased for competitive reasons (in real terms they do not represent a major cost to insurers, but they do have a considerable catastrophe potential and therefore should not be increased without additional premium). Dislocation exposures will be extended as the system

becomes more complex and overstretched. Severe competition will continue to result in financial failure by travel companies.

Packaging of Policies

Marketeers of policies continually seek to increase benefits at no extra costs in order to achieve a competitive edge. As we have shown, this pressure has certainly worked to the consumers' interest in recent years. If realistic pricing is introduced, then the current package may cost more than most people wish to spend. Consequently, we could see a growth in 'economy' and 'premium' options. The economy version would have more limited benefits and/or a higher degree of self-insurance.

There may also be an increase in 'unbundled' purchases, as organisations such as credit card companies include some coverage in their offering (e.g. Personal Accident, Medical Expenses, Repatriation Services) and other policies provide certain benefits within their scope, such as baggage and money within household contents policies. There is no doubt that, at the moment, there is a considerable degree of 'double' insurance of which the consumer is not necessarily fully aware. For example, if an individual has four times salary life cover from his employer and personal life insurance, does he really need the PA element?

Market inertia may well result in present arrangements continuing for some time, but we foresee a substantial opportunity for new approaches. Also, we must not overlook the fact that the commission/expense element of travel policies is well in excess of that on other insurance lines and, therefore, that reductions in this element can contain price increases and/or improve underwriters' results.

Underwriters' Financial Performance

Underwriters need to improve their financial results. There are three main ways they can achieve this, namely:

— increase their net premium
— reduce claims cost by limiting coverage and/or increasing self-insurance
— reduce marketing/administrative costs

We believe that they will actively pursue all courses and that their attitudes will be the dominant factor in the next two to three years. The travel industry must accept this and adjust its thinking.

Marketing Strategy

Distribution Channels
Travel agents and tour operators currently dominate the travel insurance

market. They will certainly work hard to maintain their position. However, the competition between them will grow and will result in decreased margins for them all, especially as underwriters will exert more pressure. Promotional activities will increase. Operators will be tempted to utilise their inbuilt advantage as the provider of the service; travel agents, especially the multiples, will refine their marketing and sales skills to switch-sell their products and to exploit the non-inclusive tour market.

New entrants to the market will also seek to expand their position, especially banks, building societies, savings and loans. They are likely to utilise promotional links to their role in financing travel and/or in providing a saving medium for those intending to spend money on vacations. We shall see increased utilisation of linked selling to other travel-related products, like photographic materials, tanning lotions, etc.

We shall also see increased use of direct marketing techniques not only by credit card companies but by insurance companies and other specialist marketing organisations. Affinity group selling techniques will also grow in importance. Current commission levels encourage such developments.

Role of Promotion/Advertising

Although a number of brand names have been created throughout the world, e.g. ExtraSure, Travelguard, SuperSure, ABTAsure, there has been little investment in advertising to support push-through marketing strategies. The emphasis has been on the role of the intermediary. i.e. pull-through strategies This is understandable as it is the intermediaries that have taken the initiative in selling the concept of insurance. The current size of the market now makes it more viable for major players to seek to build a more sophisticated marketing platform, especially if they can link this to their general promotional strategy, for example, Blue Cross Cares. However, the short life cycle of the policy still militates in favour of the commodity approach and, therefore, the brand image promoters still have a real problem, especially as they are dependent on the underwriters' willingness to support them on a medium to long-term basis.

9. Financial Implications

For Buyers

If buyers wish to benefit from increasing levels of protection and an ever-increasing range of covers, then they must be prepared to spend more. They cannot escape the conclusion that current levels of cover and convenient buying arrangements require more money to be paid. They must decide what they are prepared to pay to lay off risk and what they are prepared to accept for their own account. The buyer's attitude certainly affects claims costs.

For Sellers

The sellers have concentrated on their percentage and its impact on their overall margin. They have not really considered the fact that unless there is a risk-taker they cannot earn their commission. They must understand this reality; and there is evidence that they do.

For Regulations

Insurance income has become more important to travel associations than they are willing to admit. Their share is under pressure unless they can prove that they make a positive contribution to future market development. The insurance industry can play an increasing role in supporting their financial viability if they are prepared to understand its need to make a reasonable profit on whatever area it is underwriting.

For Underwriters

Insurance underwriters operate in a very free and competitive market. They are not supported by anyone other than their own shareholders. They must use their capital base in areas of best return. Their travel business, seen in isolation, is unattractive. They must seek linkages or better returns.

10. In Conclusion

The insurance industry will continue to play a major part in the risk financing of the travel industry. The intense competition within the travel market will result in commercial failures and in discontinuities and therefore the protection of the insurance industry will be vital to travellers.

The competition within the travel industry for a share of the commission income will increase further, as will the efforts of other distributors to claw back a proportion of the market.

We are now in a hardening insurance market and therefore underwriters will be laying down the terms more strongly than for some years. Insurance capacity will reduce, which will increase the need for professional broking skills. The travel industry will ignore this at its peril. It may be very skilled at the purchase of airline seats, hotel rooms, etc. but it is not in the same position regarding insurance, it must use those who are professionals at insurance.

Michael Eve has had a varied and interesting career since graduating from university. He has operated in the market as a consultant with PA Management Consultants, as a broker with Sedgwick, and Jardines. He is currently Chairman of APS International. He is, therefore, in a unique position to observe and comment on the future role of insurance in the Travel Industry.

6

The Tour Operator — New And Maturing Business

IT IS somewhat unusual, but not unique, to operate in a business where you play virtually no part in creating the need or desire for the service or product on offer. Ask 1,000 people if they would like to go on holiday to a foreign land and virtually 100% will say yes. Of course, a percentage of those who say yes, will not go on holiday that year, due to lack of money or time. I would like to explore the tour operator's role in satisfying this demand, a role based on an ability to organise and supply holidays.

Let me begin by saying that much has happened in the past twenty years and that our section of the industry is in a highly dynamic state. Changes are alarmingly rapid, and make forecasting a complex exercise. Last year's problems were of excess capacity, this year they centre on shortages. Sometimes planning seems almost meaningless as the daily pace quickens. Yet without planning we would be wandering, lost, unable to marshal our strengths, unaware of our resources. This is why I will seek later in this chapter to add my opinion on the role of strategy and its implications.

What then has been and still is the role of the tour operator in the quite extraordinary migration of increasing millions of people in the past 20 years? Why do tour operators exist? At some time a change must have occurred in a number of technical, social, and perhaps economic, areas to bring this migratory movement about. The changes were so fundamental as to require a new type of business to service a hitherto impossible dream, latent in millions of people — the innate desire to travel! In my search for these fundamental changes I found but four, and I am a little surprised to find all to be among the fastest changing elements in our society today. I will describe, and then by example demonstrate, their application to the mass tour operating market.

The Changes.
1. Technology Improved efficiency of aviation.
    London/Gatwick to Palma/Mallorca :

(Sector distance 850 Nautical Miles)
1956 Viscount : Cruise Speed 220 knots
Journey time 3 hours 55 minutes
1985 757 Boeing : Cruise Speed 430 knots
Journey time 1 hour 55 minutes

2. The Law
The right to fly charter aircraft, which enables the cost per seat to reduce dramatically.

3. Time Off
When people got more than two weeks' holiday; the breakdown of traditional 'wake weeks'; those industry-tied annual closures.
Increased parent willingness to take children out of school in term time.

4. Disposable Income — higher standard of living.
                     higher aspirations.

Those are, in my view, the elements in which change occurred virtually simultaneously, thus creating the need for a business called tour operating, a business which emerged almost overnight, re-shaping the economies of many countries. You will notice that I have not mentioned fashion. It has, in my view, played no part at all in generating the desire to travel, although it often plays a role in destination choice.

It seems to me that these variables, under the guidance of the emerging tour operator, served in a short time scale to bring about a change in the traditional method of holiday transport and accommodation. The national carriers, with rights to routes protected by law, initially ignored the potential of the tourist. Hoteliers with more traditional clients simply felt the two would not mix and viewed the stirrings in the tourist movement as a 'flash in the pan' development soon to go away. It took a new, more hungry, opportunist to take up the challenge. To charter a plane for all but some obscure affinity group was a new phenomenon. To package it with transfers and hotels was a completely new dynamic idea, and it happened less than 25 years ago.

Following the last war, the growth of tour operating was artificially kept down by restrictions imposed on operators by the air transport licensing system. With the Civil Aviation Act 1971, and the new regime it introduced, a degree of stability was reached and the planned marketing of package holidays was developed.

Package Tours — Their Growth

It is conventional wisdom that industry and commerce will boom at each end of any route, no matter, it seems, where it starts or finishes. Evidence of this was seen in the boom towns of the early railway bonanza. The same applies to the holiday charter business. At the sunny end of developing charter routes — hotels, coach companies, barbecues, beach bars, taxi firms and of course airports — boomed and flourished, and the supporting industry was quickly born. Much of tour-operating in those early and heady days must have been quite marvellous. A mystified and even frightened public looked to you to explain the wonders, dangers and mysteries of faraway places — like Majorca. A seat on a 250 mile per hour plane was a privilege. A hotel that was actually finished when you arrived, a rarity. Few, if any, of these early operators dreamt that hotels or aircraft seats would ever become just a commodity. They were, at that time, a product sold on well described merits. People saved and struggled to be amongst the privileged few who could take advantage of the package tour. What pioneers they were in those early days! Planemakers, hoteliers and even governments gradually increased their sense of involvement and joined in the fight to satisfy this new and booming business.

Like all good dreams there had, of course, to be a catch. At that time anybody could be a tour operator and many were; but in the years that followed, in the desperate fight for survival few companies developed what we can truly call a product. There are of course some notable exceptions. Companies in the 1960s and 1970s provided a more or less good basic consumer service, but many failed. Look at all the components which make up a conventional package tour and ask yourself to what degree, outside of choice, does a tour operator control the standards or quality that make up a package holiday.

1. Time spent at airports and the service our clients receive there.
2. Time spent on an aeroplane, and the operating standards and service.
3. The transfer to the hotel and back to the airport.
4. The hotel itself.
5. The surrounding environment, bars, cafes, etc.
6. The weather.

One could, of course, argue the finer points of the tour operator's role in these component services, and naturally a wise tour operator will have some impact on their quality. However, an honest one will also admit that his influence is limited. In any event he knows that the quality of these elements is of an equal benefit to his competitors. In the search for a special quality — the USP — of a product the tour operator will seek exclusive property, quality airlines, etc., and then find to his horror he has no copyright on these facilities or standards and that they are not difficult to emulate. A short term advantage is all that can be gained.

There are many once famous tour operators who are no longer operating; many of them are victims of a false belief in the impact they could have on the issues which concern the holiday-maker. They believed they were specialists; if they were, they would be around today. They believed they

FIG. 6.1. The modern image of the tour operator.

had a market but it was a market based on a myth. The volume was
artificial, for the low prices of the 1970s attracted segments of the
population to travel whose resources were strictly limited. Subsequent price
increases reduced numbers, and companies like Clarksons collapsed. Those
were the early days of the business learning curve, days when
professionalism was unknown. Survival depended then pretty much on
coping with the unknown. Today is no less competitive but those of us who
are in 'winning positions' know how to harness our resources innovatively
against the bottom line.

Strategic and tactical decisions are inseparable and are made daily, where careful monitoring of competitors' behaviour is of almost equal importance to monitoring the market. This chapter could just focus on the question of what the shape of international travel will be. One could build projections around all sorts of exciting figures and appear very learned — it has been said for example that the annual compound ratio of 3% growth may be used, with the result that the total quantitative volume per capita will grow in the next 20 years into 1.34 times the current figure. This mathematical hypothesis tells us how many people could be travelling but it does not tell us with whom they will travel or why.

To base future growth purely on the availability of willing bodies would be disastrous. All bodies are willing, what tour operators want to know (and this is no doubt why my chapter is being read) is who will people travel with and what will have governed their choice? In other words, how does a company working in an industry where the 'product' nature of their offer is somewhat intangible ensure they are the people's choice? We and our competitors seek to dominate a market where most of the ingredients which go to make up the product are outside our control. This demands a flexibility of role and a basic understanding of the hardware of travel. Tour operators exist not just to satisfy the changing demand of tourists but also to coordinate the outside variables which make up an attractive package.

Price

Let me first deal with the most obvious area in which we might make ourselves the customer's choice. Some of what I have said could quite sensibly cause a reader to conclude that I believe the tour operator is simply a broker, a person whose task it is to deliver the component parts of a purchase to consumers packaged more cheaply than they could otherwise buy the services separately themselves. It is more complex than that. Price competition falls into two categories. One is the simple truth that if you charge more for your product than a competitor, without giving added value or more for your product than consumers could package themselves, your business would fail and eventually disappear. It is equally true that if a competitor can charge less than you can profitably charge, and still make a profit, then likewise you will disappear through the absence of profit. It is easy, therefore, to conclude that a successful tour operator must, by controlling all cost inputs, be able to deliver the goods no more expensively than the competition and at the same time make sufficient profit to attract investors to the company and enable it to maintain standards of service to the consumer at least as good as the nearest competitor.

Cutting the price is the easiest of all the different market tasks we are faced with each year. Reducing the price of a holiday can be done at the stroke of a pen, but the advantage is short term. Controlling the costs, and delivering that holiday sale at a profit to your company, is what counts and that requires strategy. Not some grand theory that you call strategy but rather a direction given to well-targeted, competent and talented people charged with the task of ensuring that no-one in your industry can sell the product more cheaply than you and make a profit. One requires this direction of one's strategy, in the following areas:

volume of passengers,
buying of services, distribution and representation of your product,
foreign currency control,
overhead control and product analysis.

In this argument against price cutting, I do not seek its total demise but, rather, a more creative approach. Value is the key consumer watchword, defined not just by price but product image both above and below the line. It is the expression and presentation of values that count and this is why holidays need to be packaged to offer high perceived value even if, in fact, the basic package has not been altered. The public, while eager for a bargain, are cynical about price cuts and often assume that the cut price is the true price and the so-called original price profit-inflated.

Volume

At any level a successful tour operator will know that there are certain fixed/base costs which are not volume-related. The managing director's salary is a good place to start. If he is a person likely to develop your business successfully he won't be cheap, neither will overseas directors, computer technicians, a sales team, etc. These skills cannot be bought in ones; there is a minimum cost to providing a national service to the retail trade. Likewise there is a minimum cost to providing the skilled individuals in all disciplines required in our business.

These costs are required to be spread over a large number of customers if your cost input is to remain competitive. These are fairly simple analogies of the effect of volume — it can be more dramatic than this. My calculations suggest that a tour operator carrying less than one million passengers will certainly have a higher per passenger cost than the consumer is prepared to pay unless he truly specialises. Differences are significant and will be noticed by the consumer or through the absence of profit. It may seem an obvious statement but it needs to be said so as to dispel the frequent statement that a number of large tour operators achieve passenger volumes for their own sake. At an ABTA convention four years ago, a fairly substantial tour operator, viewing the apparent price war between Thomsons and Intasun, said that he was not going to enter the numbers game —he did not and is no longer with us. I won't name him, but I assure you he was well known in our industry. Name one supermarket chain that does not consider volume through-put and national representation of major strategic importance. I am sure that any major high street multiple retailer knows that large volume through-put achieves for his company an ability to buy at better prices a broader spread of the costs of the minimum skills required; brings down the price of distribution and enables national advertising to be a meaningful cost on a per transaction basis. What is more, it establishes national brand awareness with profound effects on the willingness of the retailer to display your product and the willingness of suppliers to entrust to you (in our industry often on a sale or return basis) their commodity. Volume is a vital ingredient and factor in deciding the per passenger cost input. A statement obvious to many of you, but more easily said than achieved. It can only be delivered via a strategy.

Brands

Although only recently apparent in our industry, having more than one brand has long been clearly recognised by manufacturers. Imagine someone attempting to have a reasonable share of the beer or confectionery market in the UK with only one brand. To the brewer that would today be inconceivable. Indeed he would feel impossibly vulnerable, and find himself at an intolerable disadvantage when trying to distribute just a single brand of beer throughout the UK. I submit that the situation is, as our company has demonstrated in the UK, no different in tour operating.

Multibranding within one company serves two purposes. Firstly, it enables that group to achieve more speedily the proper economic volume levels, and secondly, it enables it to service the changing requirements of the public more readily. Most tour operators' classic package tours are not without their stigma. A smaller tour operator can create distinction for itself, and move out of the arena of direct comparison in price and style. The smaller Greek Islands are a fairly marked example. Taverner holidays to Greek Islands do not sell readily from the pages of the mass tour operating brochure, but why should large tour operating companies be denied access to this profitable and growing business simply because they do not see themselves as specialised. Market segmentation is the key and customer demand is continually changing. It is ever more evident that our society is breaking down into an increasing number of groups and sub-groups, each possessing different needs. So a substantial tour operator must not allow his need for volume for the sake of economics to deny him access to these potentially important and yet more individual markets.

Our aircraft could be seen as a brewing installation and distribution centre, requiring better risk management and more breadth of demand than one brand could possibly offer. Many successful people in tour operating are relatively young and certainly ambitious; the management of a large group has a duty to provide career opportunities to these people, and one company or brand cannot offer these opportunities. It is for these and other reasons that our company and others have developed or acquired a variety of companies and brands that have some distinction in the market place and which can, between them, make the development of a major charter programme, the purchasing and proper utilisation of our computer and sales distribution network cost effective.

Time and millions are spent on creating distinction between brands and companies, yet we are still not quite as sharp as the consumer who seems in an uncanny way to perceive a bargain or notice a 'con' no matter what level of purchase he is making. A high price holiday in the long-haul sector can benefit from the economies of scale of a large organisation as much as a cheap family self-catering holiday. A specialised operation cannot hide cost inefficiencies behind its specialisation. Specialisation requires specialised managers; it is not a prerequisite that these managers work in the inefficient atmosphere of the quill pen tour operator of yesterday. Big companies, if they are to stay big, must face the challenge of embracing specialised disciplines within the framework of their cost efficient nationwide administration and distribution network. A good marketeer or product manager benefits from not having to concern himself with the complexities of foreign currency or the technology of computerisation, buying and administration of aviation. Leave that to the experts.

It is, in my view, a fallacy to suggest that an individual who specialises in providing, say, flotilla holidays in the Aegean is the right man to provide and manage all the highly technological and equally specialised facilities that are required to sell efficiently the product he is so good at designing and providing. I prefer not to dwell on our successes at ILG; but it is fact that up to 15 different products use the same aircraft, same computer network, same retail sales representation and are still perceived, correctly, by the public to be distinctive product-managed in their presentation and on the ground in the UK and overseas, by people who have been selected because they properly understand the peculiarities of the market in which they operate. I am not sure whether I have described a strategy or a philosophy; but I can tell you that, but for this strategy of (a) developing several brands and companies, (b) concentrating on developing top management and (c) providing them with technological and administrative support, our company could not compete effectively in the areas in which it currently does. I am sure the same is true of our competitors, both here and abroad.

Aircraft

The one component part of our product which is in every sense of the word a commodity is the seat on a charter aircraft. Of course there are preferred carriers; and yes, it is worth charter airlines maintaining high standards and not getting a bad reputation; but it is also true that only a small percentage of passengers carried even know the name of the airline or make of aircraft on which they are booked to travel. The cost of aircraft seats and therefore the profit on a charter airline will depend almost entirely on the relationship between a number of aircraft on the British Register, and the demand. Unlike the schedule carrier, there is no real potential to up-grade passengers to club or first-class and increase yield. Utilisation of an aircraft is of absolute importance. Interestingly, International Leisure, thanks to a marketing campaign late last year, has increased bookings by about 75% to 1.5 million whereas 40% of passengers flew on discounted fares last year, this has now fallen to 5%. This, combined with reduced fuel costs, means profits are set to show a substantial increase. The economics of the aircraft, its fuel efficiency and capital cost per seat, are of course also vital issues. The subtlety of securing the required capacity at the right price is one of the keys to controlling the cost input of the product we are trying to sell. It would be disastrous for a major tour operator to contract his aviation, only to find that, at the end of that contracting season, a million seats remain uncommitted and that the price of this commodity therefore plunges. It is more important to establish that you have the best price in the market than that the cash price is of itself lower or higher than you had hoped. The aircraft seat is the uncompromising commodity. It is necessary to read and understand the market if both the air charter company and the tour operator are to operate profitably. It is the startling truth that six new aircraft of 130 seats each brought on to the British Register can literally upset the price structure for the entire business. No governing body exists that can control the number of seats available. There is nothing to stop anyone from flooding the market and yet the miracle of market forces seems to control (with few hiccups) supply and demand with quite amazing precision.

Uncontrollable Costs

Our industry has bent under the pressure of the consumer press and decided that it alone is going to be the judge of the relative values of a whole variety of currencies; that it shall prejudge the cost of fuel and prejudge the whim of governments to increase local taxes and levy increased landing charges. It has decided to do this by giving a no surcharge guarantee. We often set the price of own product 14 or more months before the arrival of our clients at their destination. No group of economists would dare to be as bold. In the last eight years we have seen the dollar trading at over 2.30 to the pound sterling, to as low as 1.10. The price of oil has varied since 1974 from $12 to $30 and back to $12 to the barrel. The components of a holiday to Spain include the base cost of aviation fuel, the translation of that cost from dollars to sterling, the charge to aircraft flying over France and Spain in francs and pesetas converted from that currency into dollars and back into sterling, the cost of fuel and hotels in the country of origin, airport taxes, security and landing charges, handling costs in local currency etc. These cost elements are certain or fixed only when the plane has landed in its destination and once again taken off. Hence the debate about surcharges. It is not, of course, too difficult to calculate the percentage of these elements and convert them at any given date into sterling. Some of the elements can nevertheless be increased by governments or fuel supply companies, and cannot be bought forward. Most importantly, even the calculations that did not have this last variation, require that the tour operator, so as to buy forward, knows the percentage of its clients going to each destination. Airport taxes can vary by day of the week or time of the day, the tour operator requires to understand and forecast that element accurately. The person may stay anything from 7 to 10, 11 or 14 nights, dramatically varying the foreign currency element. The person may stay in a self-catering apartment or a 5-star hotel, with or without a supplement. The matrix of possibilities is endless. A highly efficient and sophisticated management may be able to calculate their requirements within 20%, but 20% of £150 million worth of foreign currency is a great deal of money and in recent years these elements commonly vary in the relative values by 30–40%. No other industry would allow the consumer a tentative order at a fixed price on such a variable cost product so far out from delivery. Neither should our industry, and when it matures it will learn not to. Until then, however, it is necessary for us to make these judgements and therefore we employ skilled people with a full understanding of all the devices available for foreign currency trading. It is their task to manage these in our business and they are vital management components.

Computerisation

Reduced to its most simplistic form, one could describe a transaction as trying to match the requirements of a lady in say Bradford with an aircraft seat from Manchester to a taverner on a Greek Island. A simple enough problem, but the lady and travel agent would like to know the answers instantly. The lady will need a ticket; the airline needs to reserve a seat; her name must await her at the airport and the hotel ought really to expect her. It is difficult to imagine a transaction better suited to the wonders of modern technology. Other than the manufacturers of computers and designers of soft-ware themselves, I truly believe the travel industry to be one of the most obvious beneficiaries of technology. The transaction I described earlier could be very expensive indeed and, for an operation of our size, would be quite unthinkably expensive without the help of the microchip. It means that our sector of the industry will transport about 2,000 times as many people as it directly employs, administration and reservation adding only about £2.50 to the total cost of the average holiday.

So obvious are the benefits of almost every technological advance in communication that it really is impossible to employ them all as soon as they become available. One can easily foresee several years of development for tour operators, as more and more transactions are made via a travel agent speaking directly to a tour operator's computer. Again I am afraid this function is only available to large or rapidly growing companies and further causing polarisation of our business into the hands of those companies who, through their determination to stay in the technological race, provide a lower cost transaction to the retail trade and are able to include in the cost of their holiday an ever-decreasing cost of administration. If you believe that technology will continue to advance, and if you recognise that low cost input per transaction is the core to business, then you will have, as I do, a certain belief that our business will be increasingly able to supply the aspirations of the travelling public at a price they will increasingly be able to afford.

The Shape Of The Market — The Cost Of Entry — The Future

Tour operating, like all the other branches of the travel industry, is an operation of great magnitude. According to official statistics provided by International Passenger Surveys, 9 million people from the UK take package tour holidays each year. Of these 9 million, approximately 7 million are headed for European sun spots. This year the figure should reach 8 million. In Germany 7.2 million people went abroad in 1964 and in 1984 it was 17.5 million: a phenomenal growth. In 1964 only 3% of Germans travelled by plane; in 1984 it was 18%.

The market is also highly concentrated, with over 80% of the UK turnover in the hands of ten companies. The remaining percentage is in the hands of highly specialised small companies. What is even more interesting, the top two, International Leisure Group and Thomson's, represent 50% of the UK market. To emphasise how concentrated the UK market is, over half of the licensed tour operators deal with only about 10,000 seats per annum. This pattern of market domination by a few companies is to be seen in most European countries and is a major characteristic of the tour operator business. The big companies normally maintain their position by using their buying powers and reliability to negotiate the best possible terms from suppliers. With more people becoming hooked on travel and little sign of recession affecting the growth pattern, the rewards for tour operators operating professionally are large. This assumption is based on the hope that the increase in the supply section (transportation, lodging) both in terms of quantity and quality, can match the tempo of increase in demand.

Utilisation of facilities is the name of the game: planes, hotels, computers and distribution, coupled with huge volumes of determined travellers. This is why little change in market share structure can be envisaged. Entry costs into this business are enormous, including as they do a 10% bonding of turnover, which for the large companies goes into the millions. Reflect, too, on the deposits to airlines and hotels required on completion of contract negotiations. Here you certainly can no longer hope to enter on the back of cash flow. Supplies of airline seats and hotels are limited, so market share can best be obtained by contracting as much of these two commodities as possible to the detriment of the competitor. One thing is clear, the holiday wars throughout Europe have consolidated the position of the industry leaders.

Future Evolution: Some Theories

What changes do I foresee in the market place? Perhaps, as some economists suggest, we are on the brink of an economic revival based not just on service sector growth but also on manufacturing. As saturation point is reached in the home market, then obviously the large tour operators will seek to diversify into ancillary services — hotels, leisure airlines, restaurants. This diversification will take place both at home and abroad in an attempt to have more than one cash generating source. The present demand for our industry's products is based on life styles, tastes, philosophies and social conditions. From these evolve the trends.

In predicting the future, we must identify all the substitutes for our services and where they will come from; and review them in relation to complementary products which must be available to make up our service. Interest rates and currency fluctuations are integral elements in our strategy and, as we have already mentioned, they are variables outside our overall control. On the other hand, we can encourage people to book earlier so that we benefit from the interest income on the deposits for holidays. This is something within our control. We must seek to forecast accurately and use all the information systems available to ensure our predictions are reasonably accurate.

We should also enter into a greater dialogue with our customers, relying not just on increasing penetration through sales to new customers but also repeat business. A whole new approach to the market could be set up based on built-in advantages and discounts to people who are repeat buyers. They could be moulded into a special affinity group, with regular newsletters and special discounts. Through repeat buying, people accumulate more and more knowledge about the company and if their experience is good and the range comprehensive enough, then there will be little or no reason to change.

As the structure of our retailers, the travel agents, is changing so could their bargaining power. Some have, of course, their own tour operating arms, but the majority of them earn their living purely from commissions and could start demanding other concessions. The importance of changes in the structure of adjacent activities leads again to a point I have repeatedly tried to make, the need to diagnose and prepare for structural evolution.

Every industry goes through evolutionary changes and ours of course is no exception. Each stage in the evolutionary cycle raises key strategic questions and our role as managers is to scan the environment for the answers. What is an appropriate strategy or mix at one time may not be appropriate at another. Change, alas, cannot be kept in watertight compartments and will gradually, over time, affect us all. Our industry is interrelated and what hits the airlines today affects tour operators tomorrow. We are already seeing ample evidence of this as our industry evolves and the boundaries between the different sectors are becoming less. What in fact has happened is that we rely on our individual core business, be it tours, shops, airlines or hotels; but in actual fact we are all doing a little of each and who knows in the future where the emphasis will shift? All I know is, it pays to have a head start, and it pays to be disciplined, particularly in our fluid and volatile world. Too opportunistic a strategy may work in the short run, but it normally increases the exposure of the firm to intense competitive forces in the long run.

Our business changes daily, but the need to be prepared does not!

Peter Delaney Smith, Group Managing Director of International Leisure Group, has spent all his working life in the leisure industry, starting with catering and entertainment services followed by a long spell with Mecca Leisure, where he was Senior Director for all their entertainment branches. He spent four years as a Director of EMI, developing their hotels, sports, social nightclubs and discos. He later worked for Corals as Director of Pontins and Managing Director of Pontinental.

Since 1981 he has been with Intasun; he joined at a time when the group had only five 737's in its Air Europe fleet and the single brand of Intasun Holidays.

7

Marketing Business Travel Services

Business Travel Agencies Discover Marketing

Until recently the sale of business travel services by travel agencies received scant attention from marketing professionals. It was the travel industry's neglected sector.

This neglect is surprising, bearing in mind that annual, worldwide sales by business travel agents now total almost $150 billion, making travel one of the world's biggest industries. It is even more surprising, given that the market is in an almost textbook state of perfect competition. For, even in the most competitive national marketplace, it is difficult to find a travel company which has more than a ten per cent share of the market.

This sector of the industry was so slow to develop that prior to 1980 only a handful of business travel agents in a country like the UK had a senior manager with the title of marketing director.

1. The Business Travel Service As A Product

It was probably as recently as 1980 that most travel agencies began to reappraise their need for marketing. As supply began to outstrip demand, agencies came to realise that the business travel service they offered to their customers needed to be marketed as positively and professionally as any consumer durable. As a result, in a dramatically short space of time, competitive activity in the industry has become intense and, as an inevitable consequence, the business travel product has become increasingly complex.

The business travel service is sold as a single entity. But, in reality, it is an activity which comprises a large number of distinct components. These can include relatively tangible items like the air ticket, hotel or car rental voucher. But for the most part they are intangible aspects of service delivery, consisting of features such as the prompt response of the reservation agent to the traveller's phone call; the accuracy of the travel

107

information; the support which is delivered after the sale or the quality and reliability of the accounting arrangements.

Theodore Levitt, Professor of Business Administration at the Harvard Business School and author of some of the classic works on product development, has suggested that, to a potential buyer, a product is 'a complex cluster of value satisfactions'. On detailed investigation, there is probably no better example of this than a travel agency's business travel service. Among the large number of component features which make up a business travel service (see fig. 7.1), customers attach different values according to their own special needs, their perception of the service component's relative value, and the ability of the agency to solve the problems experienced by themselves, their travelling employees and their companies:

BASIC SERVICES
Travel information
Travel reservations
Travel documentation
Documentation and ticket delivery
Passport/visa service
Aircraft chartering

ADDED VALUE SERVICES
Airfare advice/counselling
Lowest airfare search programme
Corporate hotel rate programme
Corporate car rental programme
Management information reports
Travel policy counselling

ACCOUNTING AND BILLING OPTIONS
Options tailored to customer requirements
Support services
24 hour service
Worldwide travel network/reciprocal servicing
Security/insurance services
Group, incentive conference travel
VIP services/employee travel programmes

FIG. 7.1. Business travel service product ingredients information and reservations.

Later on in this chapter, we shall explore the way in which the business travel product is adapted to the customer's needs in the selling activity. But first we should deal with the process of product development and show how it has become increasingly important for travel agents to differentiate their own products, which are continuously in danger from either replication by competitors or outright commoditisation.

Effective product development demands that each component of the complex business travel service is disentangled, scrutinised, measured against the competition, systematically improved and then successfully reintegrated into the total product offer. In their product development activities, the most professional business travel agents on both sides of the Atlantic have, wittingly or not, remained very close to Levitt's principles on product differentiation.

Levitt uses a hierarchy of four different levels of product development ranging from the most basic Generic, through the Expected and Augmented, to the Potential product.

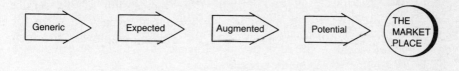

FIG. 7.2

Generic Product

This is the 'table stake', the minimum necessary ingredients which are required at the outset if the producer is to enter the 'game'. This level of product has no competition viability on its own.

For a travel agent, it means having a IATA licence to hold and issue airline tickets.

Expected Product

The expected product is just that: it represents the customer's minimal expectations. Competing sellers seek to fulfil their client's expectations by distinguishing their offerings from one another. Delivery, pricing, quantity, format and product content must all be at a level which will ensure market acceptance.

For the travel agent, the premises must look adequate for the job. The staff must have a basic level of competence. Even if the tickets — which the licence in the generic product enables the agent to hold and issue — are handwritten, they must still be totally correct in stated routes, times and prices.

Augmented Product

Nowadays, the progressive marketing of services means more than merely providing the customer with the bare essentials. There must be effective product differentiation. The basic service can be augmented to offer the potential client a sophisticated and persuasive product, making the client much more amenable to purchase. An augmented product of this kind is a unique feature of relatively mature markets.

Potential Product

This level consists of everything which is potentially feasible to attract and hold a customer and often occurs with a significant change of market conditions, for example the sudden availability of new technology.

Apart from the features described above, it would be reasonable to expect that the reservation includes a boarding pass for the client's favourite seat selection, e.g. aisle/no smoking/front of cabin, details of which had been previously supplied in response to a travel agent's questionnaire. This information would be stored in the travel agency's own database and used each time the customer made a reservation.

Competition forces suppliers in the marketplace into a constant search for new ways to differentiate themselves and move their products up the hierarchy. As a result, today's potential product could easily become the bare generic offering in five years time.

The long-term survivors in the business travel agency marketplace will be those companies who can demonstrate the inclination and resources to keep investing in the process of differentiation.

Travel Management Services are the ultimate form of business travel product development

The current absolute forms of product differentiation in the business travel marketplace are probably the travel management services (TMS) piloted by companies in the US like Woodside, Gelco and American Express.

In a TMS regime, the customer corporation is looking for total management of the entire business travel activity, a system which covers a large number of distinctly separate, travel-related activities. In articulating its offering to potential customers American Express has termed the process 'The Travel Cycle'.

Each of the stages in the travel cycle involves a subset of processes which the TMS company can develop and refine to improve the service it delivers to the customer.

- The first is Travel Policy Making — defining the rules by which employees travel and how arrangements should be made.
- Next are Travel Arrangements — which includes the logistics of finding the best rates and fares. Increasingly, at this stage, the travel agent monitors adherence to corporate travel policy and creates a management information stream.
- The cycle continues with the Trip itself, when travellers need high quality travel services, a convenient, secure way to pay expenses and the flexibility to change the itinerary and lodging en-route.

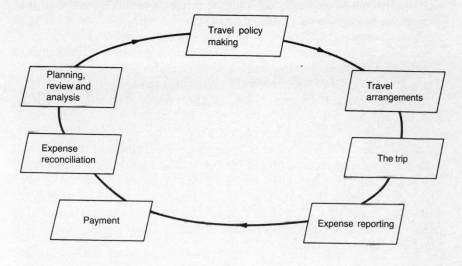

FIG. 7.3

- After the Trip comes Expense Reporting, Payment and Reconciliation. During these phases companies are looking for processes which provide either ease of administration or reassurance that the Company's financial assets are being managed properly and efficiently. Some will look for employee adherence to company policy, others to maximise their cash flows by extending their credit situations to the maximum.
- Ideally, the cycle concludes with Review and Analysis and Planning. This phase gives the company the management information necessary to help it maximise corporate rate benefits, plan its t & e budget or modify its travel policy.

There are certain minimum criteria for entry into the Travel Management Service marketplace. For example, a company must have invested or be prepared to invest its capital in producing:

- A highly developed business travel product comprising the benefits shown in Fig.7.1.
- State-of-the-art business travel centres
- A networking capability enabling the business travel service to be delivered to customers whose operating units might be dispersed across the country, continent or even the world
- Global customer servicing through directly owned, representative or franchised offices
- Excellent supplier relations with airlines, hotels and car rental companies
- A charge card system for the payment process and collection of travel data

- Effective data-capture at the point of sale, plus powerful MIS generating software to provide the customer with effective tracking of purchases and enforcement of company travel policy
- A Travel and Entertainment Consulting Service to assist companies to determine their own internal travel policies, and design and install the appropriate travel management system for their needs

In establishing a TMS approach to business travel marketing, American Express did not see itself as operating within the narrow, traditional confines of either the travel agency or the travel and entertainment payment sectors. Rather, it is a provider of a comprehensive range of travel-related or travel management services. In his book 'The Marketing Imagination', Theodore Levitt cited the creation of American Express Travel Management Services in the United States as an outstanding example of marketing innovation, a classic instance of how a company was prepared to modify and develop its product to meet the needs of an important group of purchasing decision-makers.

Consider American Express. Its green credit card ('Don't leave home without it', itself an imaginative positioning with great power), is also sold as a 'Corporate Card'. Corporations have been persuaded to issue it to certain classes of employees instead of giving them cash advances. This helps companies conserve cash and more closely monitor expenses. In 1982 American Express shifted the Corporate Card operations into its Travel Services Division. The Travel Services Division operated, among some other things, travel agencies, making airline and hotel reservations and procuring tickets.

Travel Services concluded that the larger and more geographically dispersed a corporation, the greater was the variety of its travel arrangements and the greater its per capita travel cost differences within the corporation, With airline rate deregulation and increased hotel price dealing, the less knowledgeable about prices the travelling executives, their secretaries, and in-house travel officers became. Financial officers of the corporation had little or no knowledge of the size of their annual travel costs corporatewide. The numbers were buried under other line items in the various budgets. By helping the corporation establish travel expense rules for each class of its travellers and then offering to handle all of a corporation's travel arrangements through a single dedicated American Express travel desk, with a separate 800 telephone number dedicated to each corporation.

American Express was able to help 'control' travel costs corporate-wide. It was able to search and bargain for the lowest possible rates, the lowest-cost routes, and the lowest-cost hotel accommodations within each class of lodging. It sent monthly system wide trade cost analyses to the central financial officers, with flagged indicators of deviations from the travel expense rules. American Express was able to demonstrate that, even after charging its regular fees for Corporate Cards, it could save companies with normal travel budgets over $30 million at least 10%.

American Express looked at the world 'out there' through the eyes of people whose needs it understood totally — the eyes of the corporate controllers of the purse strings. Controllers knew that costs of all kinds have a general tendency to creep up. They were increasingly concerned about the price of money. Knowing a lot about travel and travel-related costs, American Express asked itself simply: 'How can we help the keepers of the corporate purse strings to manage costs that we know a lot about?' The rest wasn't easy but would never have been done had American Express not first done what was uniquely imaginative: combining disparate facts about its corporate customers and itself in ways that yielded new questions and previously inexperienced insights.

The product and the service

An important part of the product-definition activity for business travel is the separation of the product features, the tangible constituent parts, from the delivery process or service. The value which the customer places on the tangible parts of the product will depend, to a large extent, on the quality of the delivery process. A travel agent may develop superior databases, operate state-of-the-art reservations technology or offer the most competitive prices, but these features will have little or no value if a client experiences inefficiency, delay, indifference or even rudeness in the way he is handled by the agency's staff.

This interlinking of product and delivery is commonplace in modern-day service industries. Levitt in 'The Industrialization of Service', a classic Harvard Business Review paper, cites three types of industrialised service.

- hard technologies (automatic car washes, automatic toll collectors, etc.), which substitute machinery for people in the performance of service work.
- soft technologies (cafeterias, mutual funds and package tours), which are essentially the substitution of organised, preplanned systems for individual service operations and
- hybrid technologies, which combine hard equipment with carefully planned, industrial systems to bring efficiency, order and speed to the process.

The modern business travel centre is clearly a hybrid technology. On-line computer reservations systems; extensive travel and customer databases; high speed document printing and worldwide communications capabilities, are all evidence of how rapidly and extensively the travel retailing process has become industrialised.

It also seems inevitable that business travel centres will become even larger. In the late 1970s, the 'large' units which Woodside and American Express operated in the US had an average staff of 80. By the mid 1980s, the average was 250 staff and this is being continually expanded by management. This is probably because it is only when travel agencies begin to approach this size that scale productivities start to become available to the travel company. The operating efficiencies tend to show up primarily through the reduction of overhead costs, via:

- better utilisation of central processors and peripheral equipment, e.g. ticket printers
- specialised functions such as centralised hotel reservations, lowest airfare searching, database management
- night time operating: service can be expanded to 24 hours since these staff can also supervise 'through-the-night' running of ticket and documentation printing, management reports, etc.
- more mobility of the labour pool. Staff can be moved to cope with operating bottlenecks
- rent costs should be lower, and the accommodation better equipped to handle the, now industrialised, process of business travel service. If the company is wise, it will move to a location which balances low rents with the availability of a labour pool. Communications networks and satellite delivery arrangements will provide satisfactory local customer servicing from central operating units.

High technology can assist the travel agents (for example sophisticated databases which identify travellers' preferences and habits) but in the hybrid technology environment of the modern business centre, the degree of personal contact, which only human beings can deliver, will inevitably diminish. As a result, travel companies will need to find ways of keeping the service as personal as possible. But, even with continuous training, it is difficult to maintain the personal touch in large, semi-industrialised environments. This will expose the larger operators to competition from smaller, more responsive companies who seek to exploit the advantage gained by offering a personal service. Cleverdon, in his book *Business Travel, a New Mega Market*, does not see a future for the service-orientated, local, small-scale agency, although many will only be fully competitive as members of the larger consortia which are developing. However, the smaller agency, which is able to provide a highly personalised and efficient service, especially at a senior level to the influential, decision-making executives within the chart corporation, will keep the business even when its price is less competitive than that of larger competitors.

2. Pricing

In a 'worst-case' situation, the services provided by travel agents are free of charge to major corporate customers, being paid for from the commissions granted to travel agents by their industry principals: the airlines, hotel and car rental companies.

We say 'worst case' because, nowadays, the market norm is for most large companies to share this commission with their travel agent suppliers — a process known in the industry as 'rebating'. Travel agency commissions vary considerably, but can range from 8% to 30% per cent of the price charged to the customer, depending on the product and prevailing market circumstances. How much of the commission a customer can obtain as a 'rebate' depends on two factors: the size of its annual travel volume and its ability to push the agent to the limit by aggressive negotiation.

Airline Pricing

The rebate is the consequence of a series of price-wars which occurred after the economic recession in the early 1980s, which left airlines and other travel industry suppliers with an unprecedented surplus capacity. At the same time, travel agents found themselves in a market situation of little or negative growth. Thus, the only means of building sales was to increase market share. Like their industry principals, travel agents decided almost universally that the best way to differentiate themselves from their competitors was by price, rather than by product improvements. In consequence, the corporate consumer found during this period that he could gain in two ways — from falling 'gross' airline prices and from the offer of increasingly larger rebates of the airline commission. As market conditions deteriorated, the airlines decided to make a third inroad into margins which were already reduced, or non-existent, by granting override commissions to the agencies whom they felt could do most to build their market share. As a result, during the early 1980s, travel agencies were able to maintain their margins, while the impact on most airlines was catastrophic.

Only in the summer of 1985 did signs emerge to indicate that the travel industry had been able to regain the ground lost on pricing in the period 1980–82. However, many airlines, particularly those in the US, have never been able to regain the full premium pricing they achieved in the years prior to deregulation. In 1977, the last year before deregulation, only 38.5% of US domestic trunkline revenue passenger miles were flown at discount fares. This proportion has grown year by year until 1983 when 82% of the domestic revenue passenger miles of US airlines were flown at average discounts of 48% of the 'full fare'.

The industry as a whole has been slow to discover all the benefits of the marketing mix, but there are signs now that the pricing of products by airlines has, at last, become a scientific practice at the wholesaler/ manufacturer level. Airlines deregulation in the US has created such a competitive market environment that experts claim there are as many as

4,000,000 airfares for routes within and originating from the United States, and around 20,000 changes of prices occur during an average day. During periods when airlines are tactically adjusting their prices on some of the highly-trafficked, key-corridor, routes this number can double or treble in a single day.

In their relations with corporate customers, there are, as yet, few very special 'direct deals' from airlines. Those which have emerged are mainly based on specific 'city pairs', often offered by a carrier that is a new market entrant or new to the route and seeking to establish a market.

In the main, the airlines prefer to keep the corporate customer at arms length, dealing via an agent. This allows them to maintain good relations with travel agents (who abhor direct selling) and maintain integrity in their pricing structures.

Lodging industry

In the hotel industry, the position is now much more complex than it was even a few years ago. In the past it has been common practice for rooms to be offered at different prices on different nights and during different seasons, but nowadays an increasingly significant number of hotels are prepared to negotiate the price of rooms with frequent or major customers.

Major corporations who can deliver a substantial number of bednights to a hotel chain or single property are often able to negotiate preferential rates. Negotiating leverage will depend on how much can be delivered. If the hotel is near a plant which produces 20% or more of the property's occupancy from Monday through Thursday night, plus conferences, meetings, lunches and other functions, a company should nowadays expect to negotiate a very competitive deal for itself.

A major company which buys an extremely large volume of rooms, on a global or national basis, might also be able to strike a corporate deal with a major hotel chain if it is able to direct its employees into their rooms.

Beyond these arrangements. which are clearly exceptional, companies can fall back on the negotiated corporate rates of the principal business travel agents. These provide significant savings on the 'rack rate' and can lead to a worthwhile reduction of costs over the course of a year, thus maximizing price savings. Travelling employees should be encouraged, whenever possible, to book through the appointed travel agent, rather than going direct to favoured properties (where rack rates are generally paid). This will ensure that the lowest rates are always obtained and that volume, which is critical to the negotiation process, is both maximised and proven.

Nowadays, all of the larger multiple travel agents (American Express, Thomas Cook and Woodside, for example) have negotiated superior corporate rates giving significant savings over regular corporate rates.

A typical range of the hotel prices offered to commercial accounts is illustrated in the following figure. (The figures are illustrative only; there are wide variations from country to country and even from property to property.)

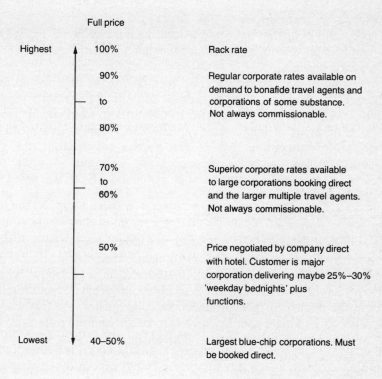

FIG. 7.4

Car rental

The car rental suppliers operate a similar tariff structure although the distribution of supply points is less complicated than for lodging industry. Corporate-rate deals tend to be related strictly to volume, although they are sometimes offered by companies wishing to achieve prestige or secure exclusivity.

Car hire companies will also allow up to 30% discount to the very largest commercial accounts, but most offer only 5–10% commission to the travel agents if they act as the reservation channel for these transactions. At the time of writing there seem to be some initiatives under way to restore car rental pricing to net, rather than discounted, pricing.

Because of the low levels of commission paid to travel agents, many of the multiples are now prepared to sacrifice the revenue from car rental reservations and rebate their commissions to the customer in exchange for the earnings they will receive from airline ticket sales.

Travel agents' commission — the future

It now seems clear that the commission which travel agents receive from their suppliers for distributing their product has a limited future as a pricing revenue mechanism.

A travel agent who receives a fixed commission of 10% for selling an airline ticket will earn a gross revenue of $10 on a $100 shuttle flight, or $250 for a $2,500 Concorde flight from New York to London, for more or less the same input of labour and capital. This seems a very inequitable method of remuneration. All of the parties involved in the travel distribution process — principal, agent and customer — seem to be approaching the same conclusion: that a method of pricing based on a transaction fee will be the way of the future. Under this regime, pricing would be determined by the wholesale cost plus the agency's operating expenses.

Travel agents, who are generally slow to welcome revolutionary changes of this sort, will only have themselves to blame when a new pricing regime arrives. Over the year, agents have collaborated in a perfectly legitimate regime of competitive market forces to create the rebate as an established factor in the pricing of their products. In consequence, the travel agents' commission is no longer seen by carriers to be an accurate reflection of the costs of distributing airline tickets. The airlines have long since stopped holding agents to either IATA or their own agency agreements and, as a result, will now not be happy to see agents manoeuvre themselves into a position where a net pricing comes into operation. Certainly, this arrangement might appear more attractive to the airlines for, with net pricing, fares should appear cheaper to the end user, without costing the airlines any more.

Robert Cleverdon, in the Economist Intelligence Unit report on 'Business Travel: a new megamarket', suggests 'there seem to be mutual benefits for corporations and agencies in adopting fee-based arrangements' and he considers this arrangement will become increasingly popular:

> The agencies can set specific prices for particular services and transactions, and offer them as a menu to prospective clients. The travel product will be charged at cost and fees added on (from a printed set of charges) for items such as ticketing, cancellations, automated reservations systems and 24 hour emergency telephone lines. Provided the agent fully understands the cost of the transaction, he should be able to generate a better and more controllable return than under the present arrangements.

Most large multiple travel agencies have now concluded their evaluation of net pricing models. Hogg Robinson, the UK Woodside agency, provides net pricing as an alternative costing method when making new business presentations. But no breakthrough is envisaged until there is a greater understanding of the principles by all concerned and a trail-blazing customer emerges with sufficient credentials to stimulate the attention of both company travel managers and finance directors.

Another nail in the coffin of the commission rebate may be the advent of the travel management services which are being advanced by companies like American Express, Gelco and Woodside.

Travel management involves looking at each component of the trip to find the lowest cost solution consistent with the maintenance of quality. This means that the agency will select the lowest airfare on each route (irrespective of customer preference), the best value corporate hotel property at the destination and the lowest cost car rental for the transfer. Each of these reservations would be made using data in the agency's computer to calculate the lowest available price, based on a matrix of current market pricing coordinators and negotiated corporate or net pricing arrangements.

The last area to provide a potential cost saving for the customer corporation is that of the travel agent's commission. For airline sales, this ranges from 8% to 20% of the ticket price, depending on route and market circumstances, while for non-airline products it ranges from 8% to 25%.

In the exceptional market conditions of the last five years, the price of packages (mediated through corporate discounts and rebates given by travel agents) has probably been the single most important factor in deciding which travel agencies secured business. This is because price is the most measurable of all the factors in travel purchasing. It is also the factor which allows company travel managers and purchasing officers to demonstrate to their organisations their skill in securing a favourable deal with suppliers.

The price of the 'product' has also become such a decisive factor in selection because there has been a general feeling that most travel agents offer services of a broadly similar quality. However, in recent years some customers have suffered at the hands of travel agents who priced to win, rather than maintain business. These experiences have shown customers that there is a clear correlation between good service and price. The travel agency which pares down its operating margin finds, sooner or later, that it does not have the resources either to invest in good staff and their development, or to upgrade its technology. The quality of the services offered will inevitably diminish and, as with most things in life, the customer ultimately gets only what he has paid for.

Most of the major agents now run profitability models for new accounts. But agents do not always use a carefully worked out, empirical process to determine the level of rebate they are prepared to offer to prospective customers. Market forces probably still occupy more of the agent's attention than do calculations based on the revenue mix of the business. In the same way, special circumstances (such as a high proportion of aborted or changed transactions; complex itineraries; or the cost of special services like 24-hour service, costly deliveries, visas or management reports) which apply to certain customers' accounts, are not always taken into account.

3. Market Segmentation

Specialization on Price or Service, or by employee control or comfort?

In the preceding sections, product development and pricing have been reviewed as the key foundations of business travel marketing. It has also been argued that no prospective customer, however good his negotiation skills, can achieve a final delivery position which provides the maximum product features and highest standard of service at the lowest possible price. The two are mutually exclusive and the customer will be forced into making a compromise between securing the best value and ensuring good service.

It would be wrong to believe that the decision-making process polarises at either end of the price/service axis (see fig. 7.5). Very few companies would want to sacrifice all employee comfort for price, or vice versa. But there are certainly many signs that most companies tend to give priority to one or other of these objectives.

Those companies which gravitate towards costs savings or employee-control generally have definitive travel policies, a commitment by top management to cost-savings, and a rigorous control and enforcement regime. They strive to obtain the best corporate rates and maximum discounts through a very professional approach to negotiation.

For companies at the other end of the spectrum, travel and entertainment is often seen as a fringe benefit and there is very little concern about achieving the maximum price savings. Such companies will, however, look for a very high level of personal service and expect the travel agency to provide this from its larger gross margin.

Company attitude to travel management provides one dimension of market segmentation for business travel (see fig. 7.6). The other variable is company size. The larger the company's travel activity the more leverage it can apply to gain extra services, benefits and concessions from the travel agent. It will expect a higher degree of product and service customisation, dedicated staff (sometimes, even an inplant travel agency on the company's premises), its own corporate rate programmes and management information reports tailored to its own needs.

These two variables — size and company policy — provide the total market framework.

Within this matrix (see fig. 7.6) business travel companies will decide

MANAGEMENT PHILOSOPHY IN BUSINESS TRAVEL PURCHASING

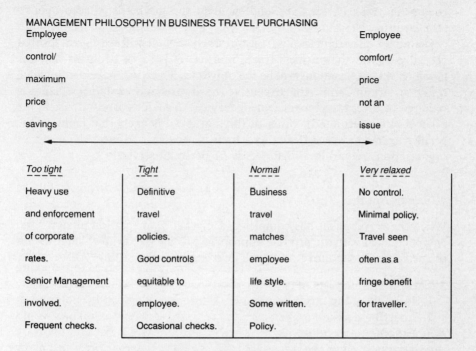

Employee control/ maximum price savings			Employee comfort/ price not an issue
Too tight	*Tight*	*Normal*	*Very relaxed*
Heavy use and enforcement of corporate rates. Senior Management involved. Frequent checks.	Definitive travel policies. Good controls equitable to employee. Occasional checks.	Business travel matches employee life style. Some written. Policy.	No control. Minimal policy. Travel seen often as a fringe benefit for traveller.

FIG. 7.5

Company size

	Small	Medium	Large
Employee control — Company attitude			Travel management
Neutral			
Employee comfort	Personal service		

FIG. 7.6

where they wish to specialise and segment the marketplace according to their own needs.

Certainly, on current trends, it seems likely that we will see a great level of specialisation in the business travel market. It is to be expected that the larger travel organisations will be the only ones which will have the financial resources to invest in the expensive hardware and systems which are required to offer travel management services to major corporations. In the other (bottom left hand) corner of the market, it is likely that many of the smaller agents have the flexibility which is necessary to meet the needs of organisations requiring a high degree of personal service.

4. Selling Business Travel

When the travel agent has completed a market segmentation analysis and equipped itself with the product appropriate to the sector in which it wishes to specialise, it can move on to the next stage — the selling phase.

This process consists of:
1. Identifying the target company;
2. Locating decision-maker;
3. Probing to reveal needs;
4. Testing product design;
5. Proving ability to deliver;
6. Closing sales;
7. Implementing new account;
8. Adopting account maintenance.

Identifying the Target Company

Different industries have different business travel patterns, and within industries, different sized companies have varying levels of travel activity. Clearly, on a travel-by-employee basis, a firm of multinational management consultants will make a much heavier demand on business travel services than either a coalmining or retailing organisation.

Only a limited amount of research is required to begin to establish the business propensities of particular industries (categorised on the basis of standard industrial classification) and the amount of business travel activity per head of employee population. Client companies and travel agencies should be able to assemble these data with only a limited amount of research into invoices, air tickets, itineraries etc.

Large business travel accounts do bring with them some economies of scale in activities such as ticket delivery or accounting. However, per se they need not be more profitable than any other size of business, because a large company is likely to maximise its perceived purchasing clout and be more aggressive in its negotiation of rebates, so reducing the travel agent's margins.

There are other dangers. An agent with only a small number of large companies within its account portfolio will also find itself in a very vulnerable financial position should it lose, in whole or in parts, a large account which represents a significant proportion of its turnover. Clearly, on winning the business, the agent would have adjusted both its capital and staffing levels to service this customer. In the short term, with the business lost and no sales or commission income to offset the costs of these investments, the travel agent is likely to find its profitability significantly impaired. Nowadays, most small agents are increasingly less prepared to take this risk, preferring to leave the large accounts to the major multiples.

There are other factors which can adversely affect the potential revenue of some business travel accounts. Aside from these organisations within the marketplace which have a reputation for being difficult customers, there are many corporations whose business travel characteristics or whose demands on the agent make them worth avoiding. Some companies insist on the agent issuing all their rail tickets. Others have a high proportion of short-haul airtickets or low-value hotel bookings. In those cases, the value of the transactions (and thus commission income) will make the account considerably less profitable than average.

Most large, multiple business travel agents have developed pricing models which enable them to determine the profitability of an individual account from the information which they gain during the negotiation process. These agents are now much more sanguine about the business they are prepared to pursue and are also increasingly inclined to renegotiate or even re-sign unprofitable accounts.

Locating the decision-maker

Locating the corporate decision-maker is the next step. This process is not to straightforward as there are many people in the organisation who can influence the choice of the appointed travel agent. There is a distinct hierarchy. At the top of the board the Chief Executive Officer and Chief Financial Officer have the key votes. In addition, there is a large number of other persons who can be involved in influencing the decision-makers.

One of the principal skills in selling business travel services is to determine who are the key players in the decision-making process and which of the bundle of travel-related products and services which the travel agency can offer best meet the needs of these individuals.

During the negotiation process, which can extend for many months, or even years, the sales person must identify and interpret signals coming from within the organisation from individuals who can advance his or her cause. Of particular concern will be those individuals who have a vested interest in maintaining the status quo or who prefer to favour a particular competitor.

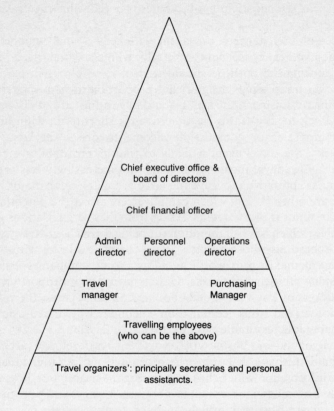

FIG. 7.7. Personnel in decision making heirarchy.

During the period building up to the conclusion of the negotiations, the successful sales person will have to deal with the following:

- An activity which is often a low-interest area for the company compared with its mainstream business activities
- Overcoming inertia by finding a reason for the company to change: business travel is only really a visible activity when something goes wrong with service delivery, or a potential supplier presents an extremely appealing proposition.
- The selection of preferred suppliers is made according to a wide range of different criteria. Sometimes these criteria can be in conflict. Different levels in the organisational hierarchy and different functions have varying needs, e.g. sales will look for service or comfort, finance for cost-savings.
- The decision-making process can often be subjective, even biased.

Probably the best advice which can be given to the sales person entering an environment such as this is:

- Start as high up the organisation as possible: with the decision-maker or a person of very senior influence. Not only will this person provide the best insights into the company's needs, but he or she will also often function as a 'white-knight' within the company, assisting and advancing the cause of the salesperson.
- Try to understand the prevailing corporate culture as quickly as possible. For example, is the company paternalistic or liberal in the way it generally treats its employees; how price sensitive is it in its purchasing of goods and services; does a strong 'class' hierarchy exist; which parts of the company are held in highest esteem — sales, operations, or manufacturing? A proper assessment of these factors will be critical in the final design of the product which the selling company will offer to the buyer.

The latter stages of the sale involve moving through the various levels of customer hierarchy, reassuring all of the decision-makers and people of influence that the travel agent is fully able to meet the specific needs of the individual clients. At the same time, conflicts between differing parts of the hierarchy/organisation have to be managed, and objections overcome.

To become the designated vendor, therefore, requires successful passage through a series of successive gates, managing people as diverse as secretaries, travellers and chief executives. The selling process involves a great deal of customer reassurance. Nowadays selling is a much more sophisticated activity, drawing on a wide range of behavioural skills. The key to the process will be the sales person's skill in persuading the prospective purchaser to reveal his precise needs and then offering the relevant range of benefits to meet them.

As with all intangible products, the sale of business travel is made more complex because the prospective customer cannot inspect or review the product before buying. For that reason, the customer is forced to make many more decisions on the basis of what is promised or implied, than on the way in which tangible products are produced. While he can be given a guided tour of a typical business travel centre and be shown the kinds of services provided to companies like his own, he can never be absolutely certain of the precise quality of the service he will receive.

This is why the provision of surrogates makes a key contribution towards reassuring the potential customer about the kind of service he will ultimately receive. The customer will be quick to make value judgments about the likely quality of the potential product from the appearance of the sales person, the business proposal, the reservations environment, the computer technology, even packaging, like ticket jackets.

Levitt has described how business proposals submitted to NASA are packaged in binders which match the craftsmanship of Tyrolean leatherworkers. Most travel agents probably would not go that far but it is important that, in every part of the selling process, the sales people provide reassuring, tangible, and preferably visible surrogates for what is promised in the service. As part of this process, American Express in the UK have now invested in sales presentation tools which include the use of an interactive video disc to enable the client to see how the product can be customised to meet his particular needs.

Implementation and account maintenance are critical to eventual sales success. Even when the client has finally decided 'yes', the account-selling job is far from over. A long implementation phase stretches ahead of the new supplier. Although many business travel sales people will believe that their job has been done, preferring to leave the less glamorous implementation phase to their operations colleagues, they still have a key role to play in determining the ultimate success of the sale. Senior travel agency management must ensure that the sales person does not lose interest. One solution is to appoint the successful salesman to the job of account executive for the next three to six months to supervise the new account implementation process.

A high degree of personalised attention is also vital in ensuring thorough vertical penetration of the account. Despite the incumbent management's edicts to their employees to change to the new vendor, there will be outcrops of resistance, whether from whole departments, certain executives or individual secretaries. The sales person is the key to a successful crossing of this final hurdle. His or her selling skills will constantly be required to ensure that resistance is overcome and the new account is completely penetrated.

Account maintenance

The next phase of activity is account maintenance. The delivery of intangible products is unique in at least one respect. The customer is, for the most part, unaware that he is being served well and his interests are being protected. While service is being rendered properly and efficiently, the customer remains virtually oblivious to its delivery. Only when things don't go well, or a competitor suggests that they could go better, does the customer really become aware of the product's existence and the identity of the supplier. An important adage in business travel selling is that 'The customer doesn't know what he's getting until he doesn't get it'. As a test, frequent international travellers should be asked to recall business trips which went well. You will find that they will struggle. Yet the last poorly executed or missing reservation, misrouting or instance of overcharging will quickly come to mind.

One characteristic of intangible products is the high number of people involved in their production and delivery: the more 'people-intensive' that a product is, the more room there is for personal discretion, idiosyncrasy, error and delay. The customer can easily be undersold as a result of his expectations being underfulfilled. And that's a danger, because the customer's awareness of the supplier will often only be heightened at times of failure or dissatisfaction. This makes the incumbent supplier vulnerable to a competitor who can always use small, visible failures to build a foothold for the introduction of his services. Thus it is vital to remind people regularly at all levels in the client company of the good service they are enjoying, and how well the supplier is looking after their needs. This makes it very important that the promises which initially convinced the customer to buy are regularly re-stated. The techniques which a travel agent can use are:

- follow-up calls;
- newsletters, information updates;
- quality assurance questionnaires;
- 'talks to the managing director' — reviews with senior management;
- recognition of anniversaries with flowers, etc;
- special events for secretaries, e.g. travel seminars, airport and hotel visits, etc;
- vacation offers.

Throughout the life of the account, the agency must never neglect the interests of any sector of the customer triumvirate — the decision-makers, the travellers themselves and the travel organisers — secretaries, personal assistants and company travel managers. If good service is consistently delivered and account maintenance procedures are followed closely, then there is every reason to believe that the account will run for at least its average, natural life — nowadays a period of about seven years.

5. The Future

In his book 'Business Travel: A new megamarket,' Cleverdon has predicted no significant changes in the distribution of commercial travel products in the next few years. He believes the travel agent will continue to act as the prime intermediary between buyer and seller.

The airlines have remained remarkably consistent in their public assertions about their relations with travel agencies. They intend to maintain the status quo. The Chief Executive Officer of United Airlines, one of the US's largest, recently stated: 'We have no plans to appoint any other form of agents. Travel agents are vitally important to us. They are how United wishes to distribute its services'. For reasons which were explored earlier in this chapter, it seems unlikely that airlines would want at the present time to alienate the agency community, either by attempting to find a lower cost distributor or by contemplating a major, direct-sell push. Nevertheless, it is inevitable that airlines will want to explore further distribution methods which might reduce the cost of agency commissions. These payments are a colossal expense for the airlines. The Eno Foundation for Transportation's Report on Airline Deregulation calculated that the commissions paid to airlines in the United States reached $2.4 billion in 1983 and represented 6.9% of total airline operating expense. These figures have changed substantially since airline deregulation. In 1977 commission payments totalled $732 million and represented only 4.5% of airline operating expense.

The cost of commissions paid to travel agents has grown because their share in the reservations market has grown, and the airlines have no one to blame for this but themselves. As a deregulation in the USA created unprecedented pricing options, so the confused flying public turned to the travel agent to perform the role of honest broker. As a result, air bookings via travel agents have grown from around 55% in 1978, the year prior to deregulation, to 75% in 1984.

Many experts like Cleverdon see the trend continuing. There may be a lesson here for those airlines in Europe which are considering embracing deregulation. Freedom of pricing and route selection may offer the chance to increase market share, but what will the effect be on distribution costs?

One alternative distribution opportunity has so far been almost universally declined. This is the option to deal directly with major corporations and offer them a price advantage in return for a guaranteed volume of business. IATA regulations prevent this practice in Europe, and in the USA deals of this kind remain very much the exceptions — despite the oft-cited cases of Delta's deal with General Electric, Eastern's with the Harris Corporation and, more recently, Lockheed's arrangements with several companies. For the present, airlines seem to have reached the conclusion that business travel is not a discretionary purchase, that demand is relatively fixed and, as a result, premium pricing should be maintained for as long as possible.

If long term changes do occur, it is more likely that the airline will turn to combinations of new electronic distribution facilities and their frequent-flyer programmes to encourage direct purchase by the individual employee.

The frequent-flyer programmes, as practised in the US, have encouraged significant shifts in brand loyalty, particularly in the early years of their operation. American Airlines, who initiated the concept with their American Advantage programme in 1981, were quickly followed by TWA, United, Pan Am and many others. There has also been a significant number of reciprocal arrangements, generally between non-competitive carriers, as well as tie-ins with hotels and car-rental companies. United's purchase of Hertz and their chance to link up with their own Westin Hotel chain subsidiary provide a unique opportunity for a totally integrated, business-travel, crossing-marketing operation.

A similar concept of total management has been created in Scandinavia by SAS. The airline owns travel agents and hotels, as well as the airline. Jan Carlzon, their Chief Executive, has a vision in which the premium business travel passenger never leaves SAS's hands. He or she would be provided with limousine transfer into an SAS hotel. The practice will be repeated for the return journey except that there is the added benefit of baggage check-in not at the airport kerbside, but with the hotel concierge. It is this kind of initiative (which is totally permissible under IATA regulations) which business travellers who need a prompt and convenient service will relate to, and reward with their custom.

It would be difficult for any chief financial officer or corporate travel department to argue that the traveller has achieved any monetary advantage from the SAS arrangement. However, there has been a good deal of debate in the US about the ethics of the frequent-flyer programmes. Although a great many turn a blind eye, the corporate view held by a number of firms is that employee should not exploit the company for his or her own benefit and that bonuses should accrue to the corporation and not to the individual. Carriers, on the other hand, will continue to prefer to see the bonus travel points accumulated by individuals rather than corporations, thus preserving a trading relationship based on brand loyalty.

To provide an alternative appeal, certain travel agents — primarily Woodside, Gelco and American Express — have developed new travel management proposals. These are designed to provide corporations with travel services at a reduced cost as an alternative to allowing employees the freedom to make their own purchases. In particular, the service would guarantee the lowest logical fare or applicable corporate rate. Because they are based on the application of precisely developed corporate travel policies, make use of software which takes the bias out of the airline systems, and provide and manage information reports which monitor employee aberration or abuse, such travel management systems will enable the corporations (who at the end of the day are underwriting the cost of travel) to regain control of the purchasing decision process.

This discrete tussle between the airline (and other travel principals) which target the employee and the travel agent who gears his support effort to the cooperation, could well be the main focus for business travel marketing over the next few years. However, the changes which take place are likely to be subtle in application, since all parties recognise their interdependence and will be concerned not to create short-term disruption in the distribution process. A key factor in this imminent 'invisible war' will be the ability of the individual protagonists to invest in the technology which will enable them to best meet the needs of their targeted customers. Combinations of the resources described below will be developed and applied to the customer in the appropriate distribution channel.

The long-term competing systems which could result from these developments might look like fig. 7.8.

Other travel agents — and particularly those who do not have the resources of the major multiples to invest in independent computer systems

By the airlines	By the travel agent
○ Toll free telephone numbers ○ Biased reservations systems ○ Traveller profiles ○ Mileage bonus programmes ○ Tie ups with cruise/vacation operations ○ Airport ticket/boarding pass printers ○ Airline credit card payment programmes	○ Direct lines (paid for by agent) ○ 'Debiasing' software/lowest airfare/price searching system ○ Traveller profiles ○ Rebates to corporations ○ Management Information systems ○ Office workstation 'ticket' printing ○ Special credit arrangements

FIG. 7.8. Potential distribution strategies.

Airline direct to employee	Travel Agent to Corporation
Traveller calls airline central reservation centre on toll-free number Advises reservation agent of ID number which is stored in airline database. Is given flight details and makes reservation. Best available seat automatically assigned (in accordance with pre-advised requirements). Traveller given PIN number which is used at airport ticket machine where boarding pass is assigned and Airline or other credit/ charge card is debited. Bonus added to customer records. Account received 28 days later with updated frequent-flyer programme information. Bonus mileage for use of airline card and prompt payment. Hotel and car reservation can be made at time of original call and transactions completed accordingly.	Traveller calls travel agent on direct line. Advise reservation agent of ID number which is stored in agency computer Reservation of lowest cost option is made in accordance with established travel policy for this employee. Seat preference provided from customer profile Car rental/hotel reservation also made at lowest cost corporate rate. Ticket can be sent or generated at airport ticket machine. Consolidated account goes to company, payment probably deferred up to 30/60 days. Management information sent to show employees compliance/deviation from travel policy and for negotiation of corporate rates with hotel and car companies.

FIG. 7.9. Possible marketing programmes.

— are likely to become even more dependent on the airline for their product and market positioning. In the US, where agents can choose from a variety of different airline systems, there is a possibility that many agents will elect to operate primarily as a dealer for one airline rather than as a broker for many. As a result, some agencies will achieve 'favoured- nation' status via increased over-ride commissions, automation and equipment subsidies, staff training and improvement in providing servicing.

This, in turn, will lead the airlines to consider rationalizing their own distribution networks. As a result, there will probably be a reversal of the growth in the number of travel agency offices which has been increasing unabated for the last twenty-five years. There are probably few justifications for such a proliferation of business travel branch offices and, as the transaction process becomes computerised, the number of them is likely to decline substantially.

In the past, customers have felt secure in the knowledge that their travel agent was at hand, to service the company's business travel requirements efficiently. But as distribution is computerised, there is no rational need for the customer to have the agency close by. Business travel customers rarely visit their agency, and nearly all reservations are made over the telephone. It could be argued that a travel agent would improve the efficiency of his business-travel customer service if he were able to concentrate his operations in a central hub, and network arrangements down the spokes to satellite locations whose function would be ticket printing and delivery.

Following Levitt's hybrid-technology theory (see page 113), the business travel agent would establish a national/regional operating centre with perhaps as many as 150 – 200 reservations agents, as described on page 114. These would be equipped with a state-of- the-art reservation system, client and travel information databases and a back office accounting and management information system.

The only long-term obstacle to remote servicing is the client's sense of insecurity at starting a business trip without an airline ticket or other documentation. After a period of time this fear could be overcome.

Tickets would be printed via satellite offices at the airport, or even on the client's premises if IATA regulations were to permit it. (Incidentally, one has to consider whether the ticket is really a necessity: certainly its only function appears to be that of a device which facilitates airline interlining.)

If the travel agent were able to achieve this arrangement he would benefit from lower real estate costs, since non-city-centre sites and industrial space would be used; better utilisation of management overheads and flexibility of staffing resources. He would also be able to use more cost-efficient automation, e.g. larger telephone systems, computers etc., rather than operating through smaller multiple units, using telecommunications and data processing systems with no economies of scale.

The ultimate foreseeable development is the installation of a complete

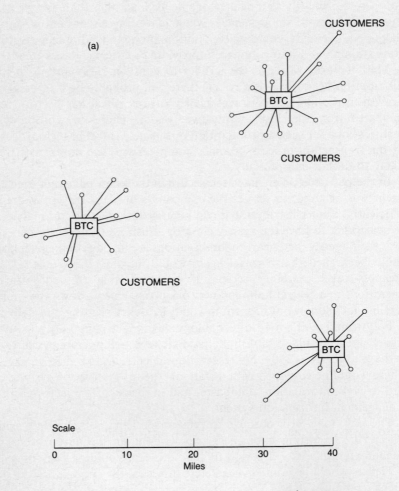

FIG. 7.10(a). Local business travel offices servicing local customers.

networking arrangement whereby all regional centres are linked together to provide even wider distribution of the travel product. This would include national coverage, peak-demand switching and efficient 24 hour servicing. (See fig. 7.10b.) 'Networking' is not a theoretical exercise. Already there are a number of multiple travel agents in the US who have sold the concept to large corporations. These corporations have been prepared to offset the apparent loss of local servicing against the benefits of uniform pricing and

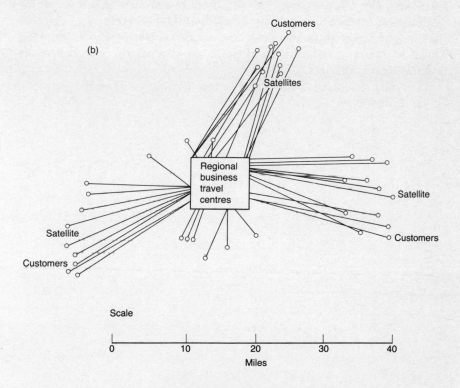

FIG. 7.10(b). Regional business travel centres servicing regional customers.

significant cost control which are gained through the consistent application of travel policy and the consolidation of business with one supplier.

Electronic communications systems now span the world and there is no reason why national borders should restrain travel agents from doing business on a global basis with their multinational customers. Chains like Thomas Cook and American Express have had a worldwide network for decades, and consortia such as Woodside, Hickory and Ask Mr Foster have been putting theirs together for some years. These agents have either built their own corporate data networks or they piggy-back on the airlines' own systems. The electronic bridging which is taking place means that London can speak to Boston or New York with Sydney in real time. Thus customers' servicing requirements are passed to the point where they can be most effectively and efficiently dealt with. The travel product offered by the international travel agent thereby becomes sophisticated global activity.

Roger Hymas was at the time of writing this chapter Vice President Marketing and Sales, Europe, for the American Express Travel Related Services Company. He joined American Express Europe in 1979 as

Marketing Director for the Travel Division and was involved in the development of the company's highly successful business travel strategy. In 1982 he was assigned for two years to the USA as Vice President Business Travel Marketing and Sales to assist in the company's re-launch of its Business Travel Product.

He is now Vice President and General Manager, Financial Services, United Kingdom.

8

The Hotel Industry:
Who Controls Its Destiny?

GIVEN THE complexity of the industry, it is inevitable that there are many different approaches to hotel marketing and management strategies for the years ahead.

Some hotel industry leaders believe that emphasis should be placed on effective management of demand and capacity. Economists suggest — as economists will — that it is principally pricing which will ultimately bring supply and demand into balance.

But hotel industry experience indicates otherwise. Accordingly, the predominant philosophy is becoming more and more realistic. Although the end-product of hotels and resorts is undoubtedly different from that of other branches of the travel industry, many authorities believe that their strategies should be similar: focusing on the needs of the customer as key to occupancy, repeat business and profit.

Price is not the main determinant of choice. Price alone does not balance supply and demand. Other crucial factors must be taken into consideration. If a hotel organisation aims to seek out a specific portion of the guest market and to maintain high occupancy levels, then it must pay close attention to modifying the products and services it offers, in order to fulfil the needs of that target group.

In this chapter, our primary emphasis will be on the large hotel chains and on marketing consortia. This by no means minimises the importance of small, independent hotels. Rather, it reflects the weight of such international hospitality industry leaders as Hilton, Hyatt, Intercontinental, Marriott and Sheraton — companies whose impact on present and future strategies trends is weighted by their enormous investment in the industry, their global positioning and the sheer numbers of hotel professionals they employ. (See figs 8.1 and 8.2).

Even among the large hotel groups, there are great differences. Hotels, per se, are by no means homogeneous; the range of accommodations and services they offer varies dramatically. The major city business hotel is different from the resort is different from the conference centre — and so on, ad infinitum.

The needs, wants, desires and demands of business travellers will change dramatically in coming years. So will the preferences of vacationers, and their expectations of a given destination. Even the destinations of choice can change widely. Today's popular tourist resort may well give way to a very different location ten, or even five, years from now.

As guest demand evolves, so must the facilities which a responsive hospitality organisation provides. Hence the proliferation of sports and recreation facilities which we are now seeing; hence the addition and upgrading of business centres which provide broad-spectrum secretarial and collateral services; hence the abandonment of the once ubiquitous steak house in favour of restaurants which offer the lighter fare — such as poultry and fish — which consumers currently favour.

Who Controls The Destiny Of The Hotel Industry?

It is a question to which there is not single, simple answer. Some would respond that its customers and shareholders do; others might suggest that the hotel industry must control its own destiny. But both answers are shortsighted, and neither allows for all of the variables which will come into play in years ahead.

If we see high occupancy as an end-goal of the industry, we fail to take all of the relevant factors into consideration. What is more, we fail to allow for shifts in product, positioning and perception which must anticipate rapidly-changing market demands.

Assessing the Unknowns: In this context, many factors need to be analysed. In the leisure market, these include:

the effect of current events on air travel plans, and on destination choices;
the larger share of disposable income available to childless couples;
the travel patterns of growing families;
and the market potential of an aging population which will include more retired people with the means, and the inclination, to travel.

The business market presents challenges no less complex. For example, the long-term effect of teleconferencing on corporate travel is still unknown. Considering the continuing importance of 'on-site' meetings, anticipated growth in its use will not sharply affect business travel overall.

The opening of new business markets — such as the shift of commercial ties towards the Far East — is another factor. The peripheral needs of business travellers for secretarial and related high-tech services that permit instantaneous communication with the 'home office' will also be a growing

Rank	Company	Rank	Company
1	Intercontinental	6	Holiday Inn
2	Hyatt	7	Marriott
3	Hilton International	8	Peninsula
4	Sheraton	9	Western
5	Mandarin	10	Trusthouse Forte

Source: Business Traveller Magazine, October 1984.

FIG. 8.1. International Business Travellers' Top 10 Favourite International Hotel Chain Survey 1984.

1983 Rank		No. of Properties
1	Holiday Inns Inc.	1,707
2	Best Western (Consortium)	3,030
3	Sheraton	456
4	Ramada Inns	582
5	Hilton Hotels	248
6	Friendship Inns Int. (Consortium)	1,018
7	Quality Inns Int.	643
8	Trusthouse Forte (UK)	800
9	Balkantourist (Bulgaria)	659
10	Imperial Group (UK)	523

FIG. 8.2. World's Top 10 Hotel/Motel Chains.

consideration. The add-on potential of trips for the spouses and children of business travellers may well be another expanding area, particularly as this option relates to special offers for weekends, holidays and other minimum-occupancy periods.

In the area of convention management, there are still more unknowns. With growing sophistication of urban and resort convention centres, and sharpened competition for available business, many hotel industry leaders will be concentrating increasing attention on this valuable business segment, expanding both the variety of services and of location which they offer the meeting planner.

Segmentation — The Vital Tool

Sound strategic planning for the hotel industry of the 1990s and beyond requires immediate concentration on several key issues. One of the most important is segmentation analysis of present and potential market demand.

Many industry leaders are linking their segmentation plans to carefully-pinpointed target guest groups; others are concentrating on developing products of specific types. But, whatever the means, the interest in exploring segmentation and in pinpointing new products toward the market demands of the future seems universal.

The varieties are endless. The small hotel; the hotel-within-a-hotel idea currently being used in many major urban hotels to accommodate the top-of-the-line business traveller; the family resort; the gaming hotel in all its

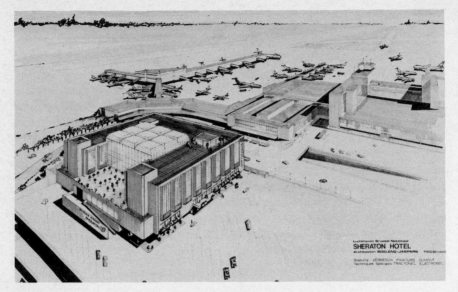

FIG. 8.3. Hotels: the importance of strategic siting.

permutations from high-roller casino operations to the family-type establishments currently being explored.

The end-philosophy is constant in this move toward hotel types, which may be easily identified by the consumer, making it relatively simple for him or her to select accommodations which fit a given need.

Middle Men

The complex role of middle men in the hotel industry of tomorrow will reflect rapidly-changing trends which seem certain to affect the wholesaler in years to come.

Competitive pressures are catalysing new directions. In the decade ahead, the sophisticated wholesaler will base his marketing efforts on the evolving needs, wants and habits of the consumer; those who react to change, rather than anticipate it, may be left by the wayside. In North America, for example, deregulation continues to spawn tremendous shifts. Airlines and hotel chains are beginning to create their own packages. Similarly, travel agents and tour operators must stay ahead of change in order to succeed in the fast-moving hotel marketplace. Current indicators show travel agents themselves to be ambivalent about the directions which they should pursue in order to ensure increased profitability in the decade ahead.

In 1960, according to research undertaken by Travel Weekly magazine, business travel arrangements accounted for just 28 per cent of the North America retail community's overall $5 billion volume. By 1983, more than half of the trade's $43.7 billion in sales came in the form of 'pure' business and of combined business/pleasure arrangements.

But the honeymoon seems unlikely to continue: many travel agents see their future imperilled by aggressive airline marketing and by a proliferation of professional agents who work solely with major corporations. To offset losses of corporate business, a growing number of travel agents are returning to the old stand-by business and seeking new ways to appeal to the leisure trade.

Although the future roles of the tour operator and the travel agent remain unknown, many hospitality industry leaders will continue to focus major effort on encouraging their business. The Sheraton Corporation, for example, maintains a reservations centre exclusively for use of travel agents throughout North America — a facility widely publicised within the trade and continually expanded with evolving reservations technology.

Increasing Productivity

With heavy investments in fixed facilities, equipment and staff, the hotel industry is extremely sensitive to the variations in occupancy which can drastically affect the bottom line. Many chains are attempting to offset this pressure with increased productivity.

The current emphasis of many international leaders, variously expressed in their advertising and in their training programmes, is on upgraded service: at once a return expression of the expanding needs, wants and demands of a consumer far more experienced than his antecedent of a generation ago.

This trend towards encouraging staff awareness of service leads to another desired strategic objective — the creation of a 'chain personality'. Current international hospitality industry studies indicate little in the way of consumer 'brand loyalty'. A customer satisfied with Hilton in one city, for example, may not make a tremendous effort to book at a Hilton in the next stop on his itinerary. To redress this, strong efforts are expected to reinforce brand identification and to create, for each given chain, an easily-identified character which will influence the customer and ensure repeat business.

Managing The Managers

The 1970s was the decade of hotel construction — frequently overconstruction — in many world markets; the early 80s have seen the results of the dangerous competitive pressures which the 'edifice complex' created for many leading hospitality groups. The years ahead will witness the inevitable 'shaking down' processes by which industry leaders vie among themselves (and with any new starters in the field) for industry supremacy.

Hotel costs are constantly rising: in most countries they are escalating more rapidly than inflation. Surging costs, coupled with increased competition and surplus capacity in many areas, have created a new consciousness of the bottom line.

Management contracts must be kept. Sufficient reserves must be created to finance future development, and new partners found.

To realise these aims, the well-trained manager is an essential asset: the professional who combines an understanding of the interlinking roles of marketing, finance and technology with a finely-tuned service attitude.

Sensitive, creative management is essential in the fight for increased service — and profitability — in the face of rapidly-changing market conditions. Creativity comes into play with the need for introducing services which, without increasing costs, encourage guests to spend more money within the hotel. Such services might include franchising space to high cash-generating businesses such as ethnic restaurants, same-day laundry service, chemists, cinemas, sports facilities and the like. Another approach in which creative hotel management is highly desirable, is building a strong, loyal base of local customers in addition to the transient business on which hotels more traditionally depend. Some successful approaches in this direction will revolve around outstanding introduction and clever marketing of 'club' services for locals; special theme parties; outstanding business function facilities.

By the same token, to succeed in the competitive marketplace of the future, effective management will be charged, as never before, with responsibility for eliminating costly and unnecessary services, such as complicated menus in restaurants where they are little utilised and making every square metre of the hotel pay. But the most telling demonstration of the new managerial creativity will lie in effective use of staff, in itself a complex art. Emerging technologies, applicable in many branches of hotel operations, will free staff members to intensify customer contacts and develop their service skills. Effective management will implement the ways in which this should be done.

Obviously, corporate guidelines will shape the direction of change in the service mentality throughout each property; but in the long run, the effective manager at the hotel level will bear ultimate responsibility for successful implementation of those guidelines in the years ahead. The truly successful managers will be those who can juggle their responsibilities to produce a profit today with the service responsibilities that ensure continuing profits tomorrow.

The Vital Competitive Edge

There is not a more perishable commodity than hotel service. Empty rooms cannot be stored against future demand. Strategic marketing is essential to fill those rooms, either by offering the customer added value, or by reducing prices; some of the most successful strategies combine both!

Complicating the question is the dependence of the hotel industry on outside factors: on the airlines, on travel agents, tour operators, wholesalers. Even as the major hotel operators plan continuing, and even intensified, relationships with each of these, they must continue to seek ways of utilising their own resources to achieve the vital leadership edge in an increasingly competitive business.

The hotel trade this year, particularly in Europe, has suffered considerably with the shortfall of US tourists. It has made large chain hotels fall back on more down-to-earth marketing techniques and turn to the local markets to generate income. In Brussels, the Sheraton has introduced the Sheraton Club International, an incentive package successfully tested since June 1986 to bring more customers to the group's hotels. Sheraton visitors get bonus points on everything they pay for, including telephone calls, food and drinks and other services. Prizes range from free airline tickets to sports accessories and holiday packages. More than 53,000 Club cards are said to have been issued thoughout the world since June this year.

Expanding reservations technologies constitute one important asset. Increasing utilisation of toll-free telephone reservations systems in parts of the world where they are not yet in common use is one practical example. Recent surveys indicate that, via toll-free phones and Viewdata in Europe, it should be possible for more hotels to set up direct links with corporate customers.

Shaping Strategies

As repeatedly stated in other chapters of this book, successful strategy formulation rests with matching the company's strengths and weaknesses to the opportunities and risks within its environment.

In manufacturing enterprises, global leadership implies the advantages of economies of scale and consistency of the international product. Among international hotel chains, of course, that is only partially true. For although the product is theoretically standardised, the environment in which they operate presents opportunities and risks that are far from uniform. Standardised operations in virtually identical hotel plants in Europe, the United States and the Far East would obviously be impossible: even though those properties were owned by the same chain, subject to the same ground-rules and staffed by management personnel exposed to hotel operations in many countries.

Individual peculiarities of doing business affect operations in every country: foreign currency laws, inflation rates, laws governing import of needed materials: all of these variables and countless others affect standardised operations. Unpredictable events, such as natural disasters or political upheavals, are further complicating factors. And the question of fashion is a constant one: customer tastes are fickle, and today's favourite tourist site can be deserted tomorrow, as new destinations syphon off customers, leaving lavishly built, expensive properties standing virtually empty.

Obviously, these problems do not apply to principal trading centres such as London or Chicago, Paris or Tokyo. In such cities, the problem assumes different proportions: how to extend market share for ancillary products, such as conferences, use of leisure facilities, restaurants and bars. Keeping guests on the premises, as we have already mentioned, requires ingenious planning; so does a parallel strategy to widen the hotel's appeal to the local market. The most successful way to achieve these twin goals is segmentation: for from a true understanding of the target market come the products and services which increase its customer base.

The Role Of Research

The role of research in planning and implementing future strategies cannot be overstated. It is the key to marketing success and the means by which changing needs can be pinpointed, analysed and met.

As technology helps the industry establish better and better psychographic profiles of its target customers, so skilful interpretation of those profiles will remain an integral marketing function. Here, again, balance is required: between the traditional industry concern with budgeting and return on investment, and the understanding that future success can only be assured by continuing, relevant research and creative implementation of its findings.

Keeping Ahead Of The Competition

Understanding the competition — the giants already on the field and new teams which will emerge in future years — is obviously essential to success in the competitive marketplace. In the battle for marketing supremacy, as in warfare, the key to victory is the element of surprise. Thus it becomes critical to employ a two-part strategy.

1. UNDERSTANDING THE PRESENT COMPETITION. With increasing segmentation and the emergence of more definite characters, by which the major hotel chains will be identified, it will become easier for skilled competitors to spot potential advantages and to utilise the established personalities of their own organisations, sound positioning, service advantages, and every other weapon in the marketing arsenal to seek success in each given marketplace.

2. CONQUERING THE NEWCOMERS. The probable entry of new competitors requires all of the above, plus some additional skills. One need

only analyse the effect of recent newcomers on the airline industry to understand how hotel chains could be similarly affected. The airbus industry, for example, was so successful in its head-on clash with Boeing and MacDonnell Douglas that it all but eliminated their presence in Africa, Asia and the Middle East. In the field of tour operation, Intasun's frontal attack on the UK market brought spectacular success and astonishing market position growth.

Potential new entrants to the marketplace may well be companies that already sell other travel-related services. Based on experience in related industries, their tactics usually involve some type of 'flank' attack based on weaknesses in the competitive position of established industry leaders; these weaknesses are then exploited by introduction of innovative services or invasion of new, key geographical locations.

The key to success against such tactics is deploying the strength of the established, global organisation against its new competitor, when major hotel chains are structured in such a way as to maximise their worldwide positioning, upon economies of scale and upon a single, consistent service image throughout the corporate network. In the growing competitive arena of the 1990s, leading hotel organisations will be forced, again and again, to sharpen the research intelligence they acquire, the marketing strategies that utilise such intelligence, their ties with middle men in a rapidly-changing travel industry arena, and — above all — the service attitudes that tomorrow's discriminating customer will demand.

J F Danielson is presently a Senior Vice-President of Sheraton Management Corporation in Marketing, operating out of Boston. He joined the Sheraton Group in 1972 and has subsequently enjoyed a varied and successful career.

9

The Concept Of Strategy Within The Travel Industry

IN RECENT years we have been inundated with advice on how to formulate a strategy. It is something we know we should do, yet sadly we do not do it, preferring to operate via the 'seats of our pants'. We read books on the subject, attend strategic conferences and, in some instances, even propound our own theories. Yet somehow, true strategy never sees the light of day.

When something does emerge then, all too often, at the first setback or sign of retaliation, the strategy is either abandoned or, despite market changes, blindly adhered to. Why do we so often fail to establish a workable strategy? Is it just a question of inertia? Are we the innocent victims of an unpredictable market, or are we terrified about being first with anything new? Do we subconsciously fear the implications of strategy, hindered by too many 'ifs' and 'buts'. Have we any real idea of where we want to be? Is, for example, Hertz just a car hire company or does it knowingly use car hire as a means to earn insurance commissions?

The answer is rarely simple. It usually stems from a mixture of all these questions and the false assumption that the market will keep on growing. The pattern of economic and social life, however, is changing; calling for newer and more segmented approaches to the market and — perhaps only by the 1990s — will analysts be able to make a more balanced judgement of where the industry has made mistakes, and where it has got it right.

In this chapter we seek to highlight the need for strategic focus, its elements, potential obstacles and the actual process of strategy formulation. Before embarking on such a major undertaking, it is important to look at the people angle. This should not be viewed in terms of 'customer smiles', but in terms of how many potential customers for our services there actually are.

The Environment And The Need For Strategic Focus
In Europe, more than in the USA, the age tree is inverting: there are fewer productive people supporting more non-productive people. This definite

trend primarily affects health and social security schemes, but it also has very significant implications for travel and leisure. Furthermore, the pattern of family life is also changing with the emergence of single parent families, a shorter working week, working mothers and a more sophisticated, experience-hungry youth segment.

Since the last war there have been dramatic changes in the economic fortunes of the industries and services making up the world economy. We have seen in manufacturing and industrial companies a disastrously slow response to change; failure to utilise resources effectively and efficiently and an inability in many instances to adjust costs and product offerings. The service industry, particularly in the travel field, could so easily fall victim to this malaise unless there is a move to re-think strategies in terms of cost structures and marketing opportunities.

The competitive pressure, no one can doubt, is on, forcing travel companies to tread new paths; challenging old ideas and tearing down traditional boundaries, often for the wrong reasons. In Europe we are beginning to emulate the American preoccupation with change. Change is equated with progress and progress with success. The drive is for the new. As we shall elaborate later, these beliefs originate from new competitors or existing market leaders, and lead to reactions from others, reactions which must be anticipated and evaluated. The inevitability of retaliation is fact, for most travel companies are market driven, seeking the same solution. Few like to innovate, most like to copy. This is perhaps why we are beginning to see only the enlightened few reassessing their roles and the validity of their strategies in the market. Often this reassessment originates from panic as newcomers poach market share. We cannot stress often enough that companies should identify what they want to be, against what they actually are and plan according to their objectives. Managers, according to Peter F Drucker, live in two time-periods — that of today and tomorrow. In turbulent times, such as we are facing, no manager can assume that 'tomorrow will be an extension of today'. We must plan, if we are to grasp the advantage.

Those of us who are ready for, and accept and exploit, change will be the winners. Throughout this book our common message has rested on the need for five vital characteristics:

— knowing what you are — leader or fast follower;
— flexibility;
— speed of response;
— assurance of continuity;
— positioning.

We can no longer think in terms of 'the usual', for rapid and abrupt change prevents that. Our strategy as managers must be 'taking advantage of new realities, and to convert turbulence into opportunity' (P F Drucker).

Although some of the elements contained in this chapter apply more to the larger firms in the travel industry, small firms will also benefit from this approach. What we are advocating is that all companies, no matter what their size, must anticipate or even create environmental change. At the same time the companies need to move forward in a controlled and planned fashion. Unfortunately, the high degree of capital investment required increasingly makes flexibility and speed of response difficult. This automatically gives the newcomers a competitive advantage, particularly when dealing with the latest 'travel fad', or technology.

Who Will Create The New Strategies?

The drive should come from within, for nothing can really replace entrepreneurs. Without their vision, drive and skills little can be achieved. However, the challenges which face them are complex, requiring core abilities to analyse the environment, see through its complexities, and to induce and pilot the organisation through the process of change. Where these entrepreneurs will come from is difficult to say; all we can ask is they are capable professionals who anticipate and utilise the external and internal potential of a company. Here there must be an understanding of the need to reduce the dominating role price plays. To avoid reduced margins and potentially damaging price wars, managers should continuously strive to differentiate their service offerings so that non-price competitive comparisons will play an increasing role.

What Must The Leader Review?

The company headed by the conductor/manager needs to review the challenges the future holds in terms of:

— changing growth patterns;
— unpredictability;
— demand life cycles;
— technology and delivery systems;
— accountability — to shareholders, employees and customers;
— core business;
— capital requirements.

Having obtained this strategic information, he needs to develop the corporate ability to create and operate a strategy. He needs also to balance the problem of getting weighty systems — controlled organisations — to move rapidly. He needs, above all, to understand his company's corporate capability.

Understanding Corporate Capability — Not Just A Philosophy But An Approach

In an attempt to create a working format for strategy, it is essential to identify, probably via a management workshop, the major areas of consideration. This is also a means of diagnosing the company's general management ability.

The workshop should use as its basis an analysis, preferably provided by an outsider, of the company's overall strengths and weaknesses and its multicapability relationship with its external and internal environment. Amongst the areas for consideration would be:

1) past and present performance;
2) competitive position;
3) life cycle balance in terms of products/services;
4) market trends;
5) staff — in terms of synergy, resourcing, hiring, training, evaluating and rewarding;
6) long term objectives/short term objectives — assigning priorities;
7) capital requirements;
8) strategic planning;
9) timing.

The 'workshop', will obviously be the beginning of what can be described as a long, painful process. It is an opportunity to question much which has gone before, re-examining values and corporate goals. The process is dynamic rather than destructive and, through full management participation, change can be institutionalised and a strategic mentality evolved. It is also an opportunity to establish a review group who will help to keep the strategy flexible, so that corrective actions can be taken and resources swiftly reallocated.

In reality, the 'workshop' is an activity which is made up from a large number of component parts; parts which help to build a launching platform for the company's future activities. What is exciting about the workshop approach is that it is more pragmatic, more tailor-made to the real-life problems and opportunities facing the individual firm. This is in marked contrast to the US strategic models which usually assume a business system and culture which often does not exist in other countries.

The Concept Of Strategic Planning

Potential Traps — People And Their Attitudes

Most of us are aware of the hazards and pitfalls out there in the market. A major potential source of concern is the corporate culture, the beliefs and attitudes of the staff. One way to spread new values is to build a team of key opinion leaders, originating from the 'workshop', who can lead and communicate beliefs within their spheres of influence. Because corporate culture and people are difficult to change rapidly, the time span of such an activity is inevitably long.

Let us look at the typical response of most employees: they do things their way; whatever gives them the least hassle. We all recognise and know this characteristic. The travel agent will usually recommend the most accessible tour operator, where ease of response is evident and efficient. Those tour operators who complicate life or create problems will be avoided. The same applies to recommending insurance, car hire, travellers cheques and any other ancillary services.

The airlines, tour operators and hotels have to remember that it is their distributors who initially deal with customers and wield tremendous power over client choice. Thus, when creating a strategy, the entire concept of service to the customer must be marketed not just to one's own employees but also to those of the distributors. Any supplier who overlooks the key role the distribution partner plays, is creating a potential weakness in his own company's activities.

Business rationale and strategy must be clear, avoiding the need for middle managers and staff to read between the lines. Ideally, a shared vision has to be developed enabling everybody to understand why a particular strategy has emerged. By simple illustration, employees can readily see at what stage of development their organisation is at. (see table 9.1).

TABLE 9.1 *Business Evolutionary Time Span*

	Evolution	Organisation Response	External Response
1)	Business concept	Organisational design Allocation of resources	Product/market interaction (positive)
2)	Initial growth phase	Increased systems, administration	Competitor/Product/ Market interaction
3)	Geographical cover	New investment Establishment and staffing branches	
4)	Diversification of products and activities	Control of branches Control of subsidiaries Increased functions Increased administration	Retaliation/Predators
5)	Life cycle/ portfolio problems	Corporate reappraisal divestitures	Environmental change Loss of market share

Fundamentally, we are talking about making employees understand why times are changing and what options are open.

Corporate Options — The Choice

1) Survival/Divestiture — strengths and weaknesses, life cycle problems;
2) Current Position Maintenance — inelastic market/defensive;

3) Expansion — distinctive competence $\Big\}$ Successful company strategy;
competitive advantage

4) Diversification — make/buy (often a result of analysis in point 1), within the industry/outside.

Presenting employees with the basic four options companies have, and the actions each demands, helps employees to understand the vital elements concerning strategy. They learn to realise the importance of the match between an organisation's resources and skills, and the risks and opportunities present in the environment. It helps them, too, to understand how the company actually makes its money, not always via the core business. It makes for accountability: vision is improved.

Strategies Of The Winners

Who are the winners? We hesitate to mention names because of the volatility of the market, choosing rather to look at the constituents of a winning strategy.

1) Low cost distribution — understanding the business, its developments and trends;
2) Concentration on customer group and sales channel — matching them up;
3) Opportunistic use of technology;
4) Differentiating the Services/Products Offered:
   which is done in relation to perceived value to the customers and the cost differentiation in relation to competitors:
   a) Specialised services — e.g. Business Travel A/C Management, free travel to airports, frequent flyer programmes;
   b) Ego products — Golden cards, Concord flights, Orient Express, etc;
   c) Standard products — Package holidays, car hire;
   d) Standard services — Luggage labels, in flight meals, terminal facilities;
5) Understanding the need for both competitor focus and market focus;
6) Avoiding competition on price alone. Constantly looking for competitive differentiation and value added;
7) Consistent management objectives;
8) Measuring performance in wealth creation and cost effective overheads;
9) Constant review of market attractiveness in relation to competitive position;
10) Ongoing search for new products/markets, understanding the importance of fringe activities;
11) Strong flexible organisation, vision and leadership.

What Must Be Reviewed?

Basically, the 'winners' maintain an ongoing review of the possible directions their strategies can go.

1) The improvement of competitive performance;
2) Changing the method of competing;
3) Establishing new products and markets.

The Losers

Let us now identify the characteristics of the losers — the ones lagging behind in strategic management, the ones who need to change to survive. What observations can we make about them?

- Lack of strategic problem solving — inflexibility;
- Limited awareness or interest in business trends;
- Too inward-looking;
- Too much emphasis on budgeting planning;
- Lack of strategic focus;
- Unclear cost and service balance;
- No real market position;
- Poor use of marketing techniques;
- Poor use of technology — lack of flexibility in systems;
- Poor leadership;
- Short term management — crisis management;
- Contradictory goals;
- Failure to monitor or evaluate changes.

The losers (or would it be better to say the potential losers) have five options:

1) Improve market position by evaluating profitability of each activity;
2) Exploit synergies;
3) Move into related businesses;
4) Diversify into new markets;
5) Leave the industry.

Each option requires some form of activity and each activity must be viewed against four basic accepted projections about the future.

1) The travel environment is changing;
2) The momentum of change will be rapid;
3) New concepts are needed in relation to products and their life cycles, distribution, cash innovation, timing;
4) The age of information and customisation.

Today, with the help of a computer and relevant data, a strategy can be

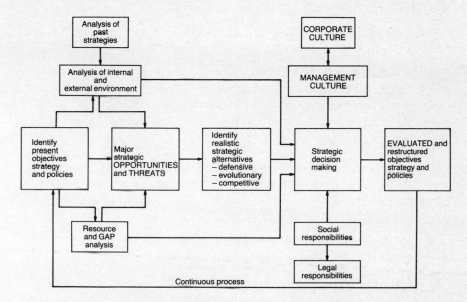

FIG. 9.1. Strategy formulation process flow chart.

formulated. However, danger looms when the strategy needs to be converted into plans and activities. Management is in many companies too thinly stretched, preventing radical and pertinent ideas being carried through.

We see decisions being taken, but, due to the multiplicity of activities and diversity of client relations, not carried out. It is too often forgotten that a main strategy creates and is dependent on mini-strategies, which need to work and develop in harmony, if the overall picture is to be achieved. When concentrating on the mini-strategy, sight should not be lost of the overall goals.

To understand this complexity, it helps to create a total framework of the strategy formulation procedure (see fig. 9.1) plus a planning and execution chart. The framework should ensure systematic informed decisions are made, programmes for implementation prepared, and should make for the measurement of actual results against criteria. A planning and execution chart should also be designed in such a way as to create and maintain commitment to the overall goals. It should clearly show each area of activity and responsibility, demonstrating how the mini-strategies interlock. It is important to note the way an organisation structures itself, for strategic decisions may differ from the way it operates in managing daily activities.

Additionally, it will encourage the creation of permanent and 'ad hoc' teams. By this commitment, performance expectations will be huge, with the emphasis on continuous improvements which reflect the requirements

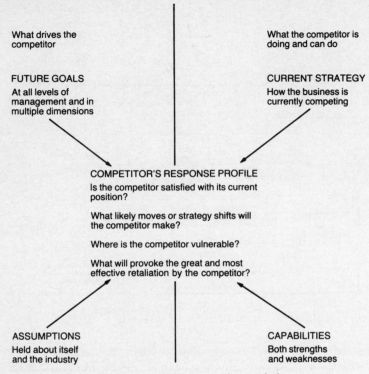

What drives the
competitor

FUTURE GOALS
At all levels of
management and in
multiple dimensions

What the competitor is
doing and can do

CURRENT STRATEGY
How the business is
currently competing

COMPETITOR'S RESPONSE PROFILE
Is the competitor satisfied with its current
position?

What likely moves or strategy shifts will
the competitor make?

Where is the competitor vulnerable?

What will provoke the great and most
effective retaliation by the competitor?

ASSUMPTIONS
Held about itself
and the industry

CAPABILITIES
Both strengths
and weaknesses

FIG. 9.2. A framework for competitor analysis.
(Courtesy of Dieter Hohenstein)

of the marketplace. If this commitment is missing, then any new strategy will flounder, leaving a company distinctly more vulnerable than before.

Below is a framework for the formulation of strategy. As a rule, during the early stages of transformation, few immediate changes can occur in the basic structure of the organisation. It is easy to attempt to change too much too soon. How rapid will be the transformation in workforce strategy? Hard facts on this subject are difficult to come by. We have observed the work done in SAS and BA, and, although these organisations have adopted a comprehensive version of the commitment approach, it is probably true to say that, to date, only the transitional stage has been reached.

The diagram shows the various stages and variables involved in the process. Each one must be identified and the role it plays understood. It must also be viewed in conjunction with a competitor analysis (see fig. 9.2) in order to ascertain an even clearer picture. From all this there would evolve the strategic plan. The strategic plan is the key document which gives guidance and allocates resources. All of us associated with this book believe that not everything in the strategic plan can be based on fact. Certain assumptions about the unknown have to be made.

We have deliberately refrained in this book from discussing the strategic

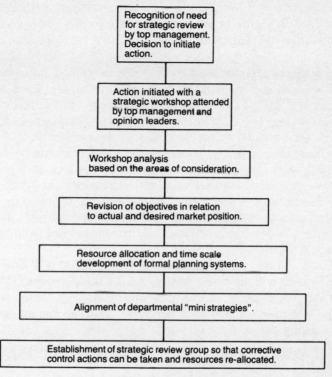

FIG. 9.3. Strategic tree.
(Courtesy of Global Partners)

plan in depth because of our belief that the only advice we can extend is that of Drucker who believed it to be a document which will 'organise systematically the effort'. The plan should be designed to be ready for any contingencies should the basic assumptions on which the strategy was built change, or if the strategy fails. After the contingency element has been developed, then a mechanism must be built into the company's monitoring and control system which will bring it into action at the appropriate moment.

What Is The Message ?

We think strategy is important. We advocate that its formulation should be managed and not left to chance or overlooked. We need it to identify and develop goals and objectives, to recognise strategic issues and to match them to our existing resources.

Each chapter of this book has sought to give, in a practical and realistic way, a variety of opinions for the future. Much of what we have written is experience-orientated and attempts to bridge the gap between theory and practice. That is why we offer fig. 9.3 as a practical methodology. The Strategic Tree highlights a timespan of activities which, once set in motion, will ensure the right combination of products, services and markets is selected.

We have deliberately omitted the element of capital investment in this chapter, due to the wide differences and needs for fixed assets and equipment etc. All we can stress is that strategy must take into account careful resourcing. The synergy between needs and capital must be absolute to harness the potential of the company in the market place. Here again each individual company, using sound research and a degree of anticipation, must create its own equation. The worth of each project must be weighed up in relation to net value and calculated risk. What must at all times be remembered is that greater stress needs to be placed on managing financial costs and risks, without crippling entrepreneurship and morale. The only limit to new kinds of financial instruments and techniques seems to be human ingenuity.

There are immense challenges facing us all, for it is a new surprising world, of which nobody is the master. As the travel industry continues to develop and newcomers bring in new dimensions, one thing will remain constant — the need for informed, hands on, heads up management. Really there is nothing else you can rely on!

Adèle Hodgson wrote this chapter in collaboration with Dieter Hohenstein of Global Partners.

INDEX